THE J. B. PHILLIPS' COMMENTARIES

LUKE

John Drury was born in 1936 and went to school at Bradfield. After doing National Service in the army he went up to Trinity Hall, Cambridge, where he graduated in history and theology. He trained for the Ministry at Westcott House, Cambridge, and after being ordained in 1963 served as a curate at St John's Wood Church in London.

He was chaplain of Downing College, Cambridge, for three years, then became fellow, chaplain and lecturer in theology at Exeter College, Oxford. In 1973 he was appointed to a residentiary canonry at Norwich Cathedral. He tries to teach the New Testament as a collection of literature, using the sort of historical criticism which helps one to understand any kind of creative writing.

THE J. B. PHILLIPS' COMMENTARIES

edited by J. B. Phillips and E. H. Robertson

LUKE	John Drury
CORINTHIANS I AND 2	E. H. Robertson

To be published shortly

MATTHEW	John Marsh
MARK	J. B. Phillips
JOHN	John Riches

THE J. B. PHILLIPS' COMMENTARIES

LUKE

by

John Drury

Collins

FONTANA BOOKS

First published in Fontana Books 1973

© John Drury 1973

Printed in Great Britain
Collins Clear-Type Press
London and Glasgow

TO MY MOTHER
AND IN MEMORY OF
MY FATHER

Contents

Translator's Preface

In 1941 when I began translating the Epistles of the New Testament I was vicar of a much-bombed parish in S.E. London. I wrote primarily because, rather to my surprise, I found that the young people in my youth club did not understand the English of the Authorized Version. For that matter neither did the bulk of my faithful church people, and many of them had long ago given up the attempt to understand the Epistles. They regarded them as obscure and difficult as well as having little bearing on the sort of lives we were then living.

My work therefore began with a double purpose; first to translate from the Greek into English that people would understand, and secondly to show that through the translation itself and by small study groups these first-century documents, quite often addressed to Christians in danger, had a peculiar relevance to us at that time.

I had few qualifications apart from a working knowledge of New Testament Greek and a good direct English vocabulary. Long before I had any idea of being a translator, I deliberately trained myself in what is nowadays called communication. Books were almost impossible to procure and my tools for the work of translation were meagre. Indeed, I was not even able to find an up-to-date Greek text until just after the war; and the spate of books about the words used and their particular meanings in the New Testament had not yet been published.

In spite of such handicaps and sheer shortage of time, the original work of translation, even though it was not published in book form until 1947, proved what I had long

suspected – that lay people know far less about what is
actually written in the New Testament than they are ever
likely to admit. I am not at all sure that the majority of
trained clergy realize this is still true today. When I read
week by week of the commentaries and books about the
Faith which seem to pour out unendingly, I suspect that
they can only reach a very small circle. Indeed, if I did nothing
else I should only be able to read a very small proportion of
them, which is in fact what I do. I do not for a moment say
that such books should not be written, but I feel I must state
my conviction that unless they are read, digested and re-
issued in simpler form, despite all the research and labour
involved, the vast majority even of church-going people will
be none the wiser.

Thus, in spite of the quite large number of commentaries
on books of the New Testament which have appeared in
recent years, it seems to me there is room for a commentary
of rather a different nature with rather a different purpose.
My publisher and various trusted friends agree that there is
such a need. We aim simply to help people to lead a Christian
life in this puzzling and anxiety-torn modern world. Thus,
if we believe in the unique inspiration of the New Testament
documents, the commentator is, so to speak, taking the
reader by the hand and pointing out (a) the meaning and
significance of each particular passage in its historic setting,
and (b) what the passage means to the disciple of Christ
today.

This means a certain amount of simplification and the
sustained refusal to enter into scholastic controversies, however fascinating these may be to the expert in the New Testament field. I cannot believe that the average intelligent
modern reader is much concerned about the continually
changing battle-ground of ascribing authorship for this or
that passage. He is not interested in 'proto-Luke', 'Ur-Mark',
the mysterious and elusive 'Q' or the various 'Johns', though

they may have to be briefly mentioned. But he is deeply interested in the historic reliability of what he reads and in what it means or could mean to him today.

We have therefore requested men who are sound in scholarship to write these commentaries, but who are concerned primarily with the pastoral value of the work they are to do. They will try to illuminate and instruct, to provoke thought as well as to awaken and strengthen faith.

J. B. PHILLIPS

Introduction

'But can God indeed dwell with man on the earth?' The relation of the ordinary world of men to another world and another reality has always fascinated people. It is the subject-matter of religion. There are many ways of exploring it, from cosmic myths to homely proverbs; but for the Jews it happened and was hoped for in terms of history. For them it was, above all, an unfolding story. Christianity, the child of Judaism, sees the focus of it in the story of Jesus. This, for Christians, is the place where earth and Heaven meet and their relation to one another is clearest. *Glory to God in the highest Heaven! Peace upon earth among men of goodwill!* (Luke 2.14), and the two come together in *the baby lying in the manger* and all that follows. Luke's overriding aim is precisely this: to 'earth' the gospel of the kingdom by weaving it into the mundane, everyday world of men and time. He connects the poetry and the prose. This is what so strongly attracted Rembrandt to him when he moved religious painting away from the Italian grand manner and into the realities of street-life and home-life in Amsterdam. And this can still capture and move the modern reader.

THE NATURE OF LUKE'S BOOK

Something like it had already been done. Paul's fundamental message was the story of Jesus' death and resurrection, but Mark was the first to take the momentous step of presenting the Christian gospel entirely in the form of a narrative. There the accent falls so heavily on Jesus' last days (probably because Mark was concerned for people facing martyrdom)

that it is hardly a 'life' of Jesus at all. The fierce concentration
on discipleship to the death allows for little guidance on the
more humdrum affairs of living. Matthew got hold of
Mark's book and set about remedying this deficiency by
adding to Mark's story-line, slightly trimmed up, a wealth
of guidance on matters of life and conduct, church order,
and the status of the new community vis-à-vis its Jewish
parent. He was adapting Mark to a different situation: a
church occupied with discovering its own disciplines, norms
and theological roots in more peaceful circumstances than
Mark's Christians enjoyed. And then Luke. Mark had given
him a story and Matthew a compendium of teaching.[1] He
used both these sources, often freely and adventurously. As
a third ingredient he added substantial sections which are
not in Matthew or Mark but have a homogeneity of their
own, suggesting that they are mainly his words. His aim in
all this is something new: to present Christianity to the wider
world by means of telling its story as clearly and attractively
as possible in the hope of winning (possibly) converts and
(certainly) respect for this new religion.

With Luke the premium is on the telling of the tale – but
not as Mark told it. The mind-blowing mystery and tremendous revelation which impresses and disorientates readers of
the earlier gospel must be cooled down and passed through
everyday conductors to make them acceptable and appetizing
to a prosperous (cf. Luke's many well-to-do characters) and
peaceful world. Luke's version of Mark's story thus has a
leisurely unfolding and methodical attention to temporal
sequence which are lacking in the original. It is much more

1. Most scholars believe that, instead of Luke using Matthew, they
both used a (now vanished) document called 'Q'. But I have followed
the minority who believe that Luke used Matthew. This has the pragmatic advantage of sparing the reader a lot of speculation and allowing
him (if the non-'Q' school is right) to see Luke's work on an accessible
and existing source.

like history, much more realistic, much easier to read. Mark's terrifying Christ becomes sympathetic and behaves more like a good man and less like a tiger. The Matthean teaching material needs similar attention. It is dragged out of its ecclesiastically Christian setting into the market-place, there to commend itself as inspired common sense or 'wisdom'. Anything that does not survive the move simply disappears. These two dominant tendencies which govern Luke's use of the work of his predecessors, the love of both the strong story-line moving clearly through time and of salty and realistic teaching, come right into the open in the sections which are his alone. No Christian stories are as well done or successful as his first chapters (Christmas as we know it is virtually a Lucan affair) or the walk to Emmaus in the last chapter. The care for the least and the lost (vestigially present in Mark, a distinct feature of church life in Matthew) emerges in Luke as the whole gospel, the specifically Christian thing. The stories of the Good Samaritan and the Prodigal Son combine the good story and the universal moral with unforgettable force. There may well be sources other than the Old Testament and its Apocrypha behind these famous passages of Luke's, but this commentary has to leave aside those speculations and concentrate instead on the skill with which Luke presents them and the many features which they have in common.

Luke's achievement was to write a secular gospel: the eternal God revealed in a developing story tied into human time and character, bound into the history and fate of the Jews and the church, declaring himself in an ethical demand for compassion, reconciliation and decision-for-the-good which nobody could mistake or evade. He has done it so well (so plausibly, to put it slightingly) that most reconstructions of Jesus' character and history lean heavily on his work – even when done by those who know very well that this is not the earliest of the first three gospels. Jesus the prophet to the Jews, the man for others, the graphic teacher of everyday realities, the man of prayer and peace – all these are hinted at in the other gospels, but reach their definitive clarity in Luke. Yet this, most people like to feel, rather than Mark's earlier picture, is how it must have been (or, again slightingly, how they would prefer it to have been). Luke has won the battle for the Christian mind and particularly for the liberal Christian mind.

THE NATURE OF THIS COMMENTARY

Gramophone records have notes on their sleeves designed to sharpen the listener's appreciation by picking out the themes in the music and showing how they are developed and given new twists as the work goes along. That is just what has been attempted here. To get the most out of the book the reader should be ready, like the devotee of Wagner's operas, for motifs like Jerusalem, repentance, the journey and the supper table to come up repeatedly – with differences. This way of looking at the book is certainly biased: it presupposes a good measure of imaginative and creative skill on the part of the evangelist. It treats him seriously as a writer and is more concerned to look for signs of his techniques and favourite subjects than for the pure historical facts behind it. Luke owed much to the story-telling traditions of the Old Testament and its Apocrypha, so the reader would do well to read something like the Joseph stories, Jonah or Tobit before getting down to Luke. This will admit him to that world of the evangelist where fact and fable were inseparable. It will also awaken the appetite for listening to a story for its own sake which will increase his enjoyment of a writer who is more of a story-teller than an historian in the modern scientific sense.

References to the Old Testament and the first two gospels are included when they are important. The reader will miss something if he does not trouble to look them up. A lively sense of the character of any work of art comes about largely by comparing and contrasting it with similar and related works.

So here is a commentary that is primarily on Luke. What about Jesus? He is behind it all, but between him and us stands the evangelist. This is not a disadvantage. The believer learns about God and the 'other reality' by studying for their own sake those people, happenings or ideas which point to God in their very different ways. Only so does he come to his own view and become a pointer for others. So with Jesus. One has to listen to his gospel according to Paul, John, Matthew, Mark and Luke; and by appreciating these very different witnesses, each for his own sake, come to one's own particular conviction and witness concerning him. With Luke most of the conviction and the witness comes through the story and the stories. Some of these are certainly legend or, in modern terminology, fiction.[2] It is my firm conviction that this does not allow us to take them any less seriously – either historically, as belonging to the New Testament exploration of the meaning of the presence of God in Jesus of Nazareth, or morally as indicating the possibilities and duties of human existence. It is a shallow form of enlightenment, with its own sad penalties, which has no use for the truths of disciplined imagination. And I wonder whether critics who look askance at the perennial human appetite for making stories and listening to them have not ignored one of the foremost ways in which we begin to know God. The commentary aims only to help the reader attend to the tale, and leaves him to make his own conclusions.

2. It is the same in the Jewish histories of the Old Testament and its Apocrypha which taught Luke his trade.

I

Introductory

1. 1–4

Dear Theophilus,

1   Many people have already written an account of the events which have happened among us,

2   basing their work on the evidence of those who, we know, were eye-witnesses as well as teachers of the message.

3   I have therefore decided, since I have traced the course of these happenings carefully from the beginning, to set them down for you myself in their proper order,

4   so that you may have reliable information about the matters in which you have already had instruction.

The other three gospel-writers plunge straight into their work, but Luke is more leisurely and ceremonious. He begins in a civilized way with the sort of preface which readers of the time were used to finding at the opening of historical books. He introduces himself and his work in two carefully articulated sentences – a cultivated performance which his cultivated readers will have relished and admired. Theophilus means 'God-friend' and so includes any devout reader. Whether or not there was a real Theophilus, Luke certainly wrote for a public and not one person.

But there is more to the sentence than polite incantation. Two things at least are clear.

1. Luke is not the first in the field. *Many people have already written an account of the events which have happened among us* (i.e. the Christians). He stands, then, at some distance from the events which he is going to tell us about and he is aware of it.

Between the 'now' of Luke's writing and the 'then' of the events which happened stand the *many* writers, the *eye-witnesses* and the *teachers* who have shaped and developed the message. Luke did not have direct access to the facts any more than we do. He must rely on others. He is writing about another time which is some way away from him, the time of the life of Jesus. Already it is an old and sacred story.

2. So why is Luke telling it over again? He has his own answer: *to set them* (the events) *down . . . in their proper order,* (or in an orderly and connected narrative) *so that you may have reliable information about the matters in which you have already had instruction.* Other people have been at work already, so the reader knows something of the Christian gospel. Luke's aim is to fill this out and order it, and he sets about it in a particular way. He is not going to do it by propositions and arguments like Paul, nor in great visions of the future like the writer of Revelation. He is going to tell a story. He is doing so because it was in a story that it happened. Jesus lived a certain kind of life (summarized by Luke in Peter's sermon in Acts 10.38: 'how God anointed him with the Holy Spirit and with power. He went about doing good and healing all who were oppressed by the devil, for God was with him'). He died on the cross and was raised to new life. There would be no Christianity without these *events which have happened.* But Luke is not neutral or dispassionate. He also tells the story because he wants his audience to enter into it and take it into their systems and their living. He wants his readers to become disciples or at least admirers of Jesus by reading his book. So Luke has an eye on the past (verse 1) and on the present of his readers (verse 4). For this reason he has sifted through the material which lies between those two points, the tradition of *eye-witnesses* and *teachers of the message.* He has recast it all in the form of an orderly and connected narrative which keeps things moving along and takes with it anyone who likes to listen to a story and lose himself in it.

2

As the Darkness Clears Away

'Why hast thou cast us off, O God? Is it for ever?
Why art thou so stern, so angry with the sheep of thy flock?
    Remember the assembly of thy people,
    taken long since for thy own,
and Mount Zion, which was thy home . . . .
We cannot see what lies before us, we have no prophet now,
    we have no one who knows how long this is to last.'

(Psalm 74)

The story begins in Jerusalem and in the Temple: in other words at the centre (for Luke) of religious history. The characters are archetypes of Jewry, devout old people like Zacharias and Elisabeth, Simon and Anna, the humble of heart like Joseph, Mary and the shepherds. For people like these it was a time of patient waiting, and the excitement of Luke's narrative mounts as it becomes clearer that what they have waited for is starting to happen. God is remembering his people and returning to Jerusalem (Mount Zion), his home. An outbreak of angels in unlikely places heralds his coming. The darkness of generations clears away, happy voices break into the silence, and the aching void starts to fill with the presence of God.

Like this gospel's first sentence, its first chapters are beautifully constructed. The Old Testament, Luke's Bible, is the primary surviving source of both style and content. Luke begins by stating two themes or starting two stories: John will be born, Jesus will be born. Then he brings the two together: Mary and Elisabeth meet. They separate again: John is born, Jesus is born. After this he drops his two-fold pattern because Jesus is, after all, the centre of his gospel and not John. He adds three stories about Jesus at different stages of his life: the shepherds at his birth, his religious initiation, his adolescence. The last two are set in Jerusalem, like the opening story of Zacharias. Inside these schemes Luke works out a number of themes and motifs. He is concerned with relations: of John to Jesus, of the neglected corners of human existence to its centre, and above all with the relation of the new gospel and the old Jewish religion. Except for the songs, where the underlying theology bursts out in prayer and praise, all this is done in narrative form.

I. 5–25

5   The story begins in the days when Herod was king of Judaea with a priest called Zacharias (who belonged to the Abijah section of the priesthood), whose wife Elisabeth was, like him, a descendant of Aaron.

6   They were both truly religious people, blamelessly observing all the Lord's commandments and requirements.

7   They were childless through Elisabeth's infertility, and both of them were getting on in years.

8   One day, while Zacharias was performing his priestly functions (it was the turn of his division to be on duty),

9   it fell to him to go into the sanctuary and burn the incense.

10   The crowded congregation outside was praying at the actual time of the incense-burning,

11   when an angel of the Lord appeared on the right side of the incense-altar.

12   When Zacharias saw him, he was terribly agitated and a sense of awe swept over him.

13 But the angel spoke to him,

'Do not be afraid, Zacharias; your prayers have been heard. Elisabeth your wife will bear you a son, and you are to call him John.

14 This will be joy and delight to you and many more will be glad because he is born.

15 He will be one of God's great men; he will touch neither wine nor strong drink and he will be filled with the Holy Spirit from the moment of his birth.

16 He will turn many of Israel's children to the Lord their God.

17 He will go out before God in the spirit and power of Elijah – to reconcile fathers and children, and bring back the disobedient to the wisdom of good men – and he will make a people fully ready for their Lord.'

18 But Zacharias replied to the angel,

'How can I know that this is true? I am an old man myself and my wife is getting on in years . . .'

19 'I am Gabriel,' the angel answered. 'I stand in the presence of God, and I have been sent to speak to you and tell you this good news.

20 Because you do not believe what I have said, you shall live in silence, and you shall be unable to speak a word until the day that it happens. But be sure that everything that I have told you will come true at the proper time.'

21 Meanwhile, the people were waiting for Zacharias, wondering why he stayed so long in the sanctuary.

22 But when he came out and was unable to speak a word to them – for although he kept making signs, not a sound came from his lips – they realized that he had seen a vision in the Temple.

23 Later, when his days of duty were over, he went back home,

24 and soon afterwards his wife Elisabeth became pregnant and kept herself secluded for five months.

25   'How good the Lord is to me,' she would say, 'now that
       he has taken away the shame that I have suffered.'

Luke begins at an earlier point in time than either of the
first two evangelists. This is typical of his more leisurely
approach and of his interest in linking his gospel to history
and the passage of time. John is older than Jesus but sub-
ordinate to him in the sight of God. All the evangelists are
concerned to put the Baptist in his place as less than Jesus.
('Never has there appeared . . . a mother's son greater than
John the Baptist, and yet the least in the kingdom of Heaven
is greater than he.' Matthew 11.11.) In John's gospel this is
done by a short discourse (John 3.25–30). Luke, just as
characteristically, does it by means of a narrative in which the
birth of John is put alongside the birth of Jesus and joined to
it in ways which show the higher status of Christ. The first
chapter is thus a diptych, two pictures side by side which
both match one another and point up their differences.
    It is anybody's guess how much of the material here is
strictly historical, for we have nothing to check against it.
Luke would have been lucky to find any hard facts about
these obscure beginnings, but perhaps he did. We can, however, be sure of the presence of two elements in these stories
beside the questionable one of historical reminiscence. One
is Luke's own skill as a story-teller and theologian, for these
early chapters are full of his favourite words and themes.
The other is the influence of the Old Testament. In this
present passage the account of the birth of Samuel in 1
Samuel 1 and 2.1–11 is a point of reference and a source. It
should be read in conjunction with it. The general tone of
both is that of a rich and resonant fairy tale ('once upon a
time there were two old people, a man and his wife . . .').
    By various touches of detail Luke gives the story an archaic
colouring. This is not just an aesthetic touching-up but
fulfils his theological aim of connecting the beginning of the

gospel with the ancient history and traditions of God's past dealings with his people. Zacharias and Elisabeth are both descended from Aaron and are fine examples of traditional piety. The gospel begins where it is going to end – in Jerusalem, the city where God had established himself of old, the centre of the world, the place to which he would return one day (Psalm 74, quoted above). The Temple is the centre of the city and the nation, a place 'where all's accustomed, ceremonious', a place of time-honoured rituals such as the incense-burning at dawn and dusk ordained in Exodus 30.7 and 8. Angels were a traditional part of Jewish thinking and imagery, carriers of messages from God to men. Gabriel's name comes from the book of Daniel, and when he describes what John will be like he uses a mosaic of Old Testament pieces. In being *one of God's great men* who *will touch neither wine nor strong drink* he resembles Samuel and Samson. As an inspired herald of God's presence he is spiritually connected with Elijah whom the Jews believed would come again to proclaim the return of God to his people. Malachi 3 seems to lie behind it all.

So much for materials and style. They serve and present a theology. More important than anything else is the biblical doctrine of God. God is known by what he does, and his great act is to call things into being out of nothing, as in Exodus and in Genesis. He is the one who makes streams bubble up in the desert, who makes the barren woman a joyful mother of children (Sarah, Hannah, and now Elisabeth), who is to raise Jesus from the grave. In a world of anxious waiting and emptiness his dynamic presence is felt as a terrifying interruption (Zacharias, verse 12). Yet we are not to be afraid (Gabriel, verse 13) because God is for us and on the other side of the divine terror is human joy (verse 14). This theme of fear at a divine presence followed by the command *Do not be afraid* recurs at 1.29,30 (Mary) and 2.9,10 (shepherds). Anyone in God's presence feels both alarmed and comforted; comforted because, like Zacharias, his hope and waiting are fulfilled (verses 13–17), alarmed because his doubt and habitual scepticism are severely judged (verses 18–20).

The Holy Spirit is first mentioned at verse 15 and will play a determining and initiating part in these early chapters as in the first pages of Acts. It is everything that the Jews had been waiting for for three centuries, the presence of God in human lives energizing them, filling them and joining them to himself. The Spirit, being God, is both disturber and comforter (see Ezekiel 37.1–14).

1.26–38

26 Then, in the sixth month, the angel Gabriel was sent from God to a Galilean town, Nazareth by name,

27 to a young woman who was engaged to a man called Joseph (a descendant of David). The girl's name was Mary.

28 The angel entered her room and said,
'Greetings to you, Mary. O favoured one! – the Lord is with you!'

29 Mary was deeply perturbed at these words and wondered what such a greeting could possibly mean.

30 But the angel said to her,
'Do not be afraid, Mary; God loves you dearly.

31 You are going to be the mother of a son, and you will call him Jesus.

32 He will be great and will be known as the Son of the Most High. The Lord God will give him the throne of his forefather, David,

33 and he will be king over the people of Jacob for ever. His reign shall never end.'

34 Then Mary spoke to the angel,
'How can this be,' she said, 'I am not married!'

35   But the angel made this reply to her:
     'The Holy Spirit will come upon you, the power of the
     Most High will overshadow you. Your child will there-
     fore be called holy – the Son of God.
36   Your cousin Elisabeth has also conceived a son, old as
     she is. Indeed, this is the sixth month for her, a woman
     who was called barren.
37   For no promise of God can fail to be fulfilled.'
38   'I belong to the Lord, body and soul,' replied Mary,
     'let it happen as you say.' And at this the angel left her.

The scene changes to the second panel of Luke's diptych.
The evangelist gives a note of time, six months after the
previous scene, to preserve continuity in spite of the shift.
The basic story-line here is the same as before: an angel
announces an unexpected and miraculous birth. The
similarity makes the points of difference all the more striking,
and together they add up to a quiet assertion of the superior-
ity of Mary over Zacharias just as her son is going to be a
greater man than his.

  In moving from Jerusalem to Nazareth we have left the
centre of Judaism for somewhere out on the fringe. That
looks like a step backwards, but time and again in the Bible
and experience God begins his work not in the great centres
but in obscure and unrespected corners of town and country.

  There are echoes from the past. The descent of Joseph and
Mary from David matches the Aaronic ancestry of Zacharias
and Elisabeth. Although some expected a great deliverer
from God to be descended from Levi, the main stream of
Old Testament prophecy (Isaiah, Jeremiah, Ezekiel, Zech-
ariah) expected him to be a descendant of David, the king
chosen and loved by God who ruled a united people. David
stands for Israel in much the same way as Arthur stands for
Britain. Mary is 'Mariam' in the Greek, the name of Moses'
sister (see her song of deliverance at Exodus 15.21 and com-

pare it with the Magnificat). Similarly Jesus (verse 37) is the same name in Greek as Joshua, the man who led the people into the longed-for promised land.

In verse 28 Gabriel has a courteous and deferential greeting for Mary such as he did not have for Zacharias. It is as if he were addressing a superior. All the same, Mary, like Zacharias, is *deeply perturbed*. She too is told: *Do not be afraid*. In the description of Jesus and his mission which follows it is clear that he is no preparer of the way but the one for whom the way is prepared. *He will be great* – full stop, not just *one of God's great men*. He is given the most exalted title possible, *Son of the Most High*, which is to say that his relation to God is as intimate and privileged as that of son to father. In the Old Testament kings were sons of God – his regents. John the Baptist's work was temporary, meant for a certain time and then over and done with, but *he will be King over the people of Jacob* (Israel) *for ever. His reign shall never end*. No more than that could be said.

Where Zacharias doubted the possibility of what he was promised (verse 18), Mary simply wonders how it can come about. Gabriel's answer is that it will happen by a greater miracle than John's birth, by a direct and unassisted act of God: like the creation of the world when God's Spirit hovered over the abyss so now it will *overshadow* Mary, as at the creation of the Israelite nation, when God's presence overshadowed Mount Sinai. Verse 37 is a reminiscence of God's word to Abraham when he promised him a son, a word which never returns to him empty but does what he sends it to do. Mary's answer, *I belong to the Lord, body and soul, let it happen as you say* (A.V. 'Behold the handmaid of the Lord; be it unto me according to thy word.') is the perfect and classical human response to God, the shortest and best prayer for all readers and hearers of the Bible. It expresses the dignified obedience, withholding nothing, which lets God into his world.

The remarks which were made about the theology of the

previous passage apply here too. There is no judgment on Mary because, unlike Zacharias, she offers no opposition to God's purposes. As a result the atmosphere is calmer and more clearly fulfilled. Mary and Gabriel are at home with one another in a ceremonious way.

A new element in the theology is introduced – the nature and destiny of Jesus. As *Son of the Most High* he is God's right-hand man. He is the fulfilment of all the hints and promises of previous centuries, his influence stretches through the future into eternity.

Since it gives difficulty to many people, something should be said about the virgin birth. Those who have no difficulty over it need read no further – granted that their ability to swallow it is equalled by their grasp of its meaning! In these birth stories we are in a region more legend than history. In legends and fairy tales ideas are put in the form of drama and event (cf. 'The Sleeping Beauty' which is the doctrine of redemption played out). Abstract doctrine has no place. It is absorbed in the action. So here, the Christian conviction that Jesus stands out from humanity by his outstandingly close and lively relationship with God is dramatized by his actually being God's son. The Christian belief that Jesus is a new beginning for us is acted out here by his birth being an interruption of the continuity of human generations, conceived of the Holy Spirit. It could be suggested that the virgin birth is a reading back into the beginning of Jesus' life of its culmination, the resurrection. The pattern of both events is the same, both combine myth and history, and it was the resurrection which showed Jesus as a new beginning and not a dead end, God's son in the resurrecting and radically renewing power of the Spirit. The danger, which the church had to cope with later, is that the virgin birth makes Jesus too different and takes him away from us – but Luke is not bothered with this.

The scene before us has appealed to ordinary people and

to artists of all ages, because it actualizes the meeting of
Heaven and earth, of the ordinary and the ideal, which life
and art struggle for.

1.39–56

39   With little delay Mary got ready and hurried off to the
hillside town in Judaea where Zacharias and Elisabeth
lived.

40   She went into their house and greeted Elisabeth.

41   When she heard Mary's greeting, the unborn child
stirred inside her and she herself was filled with the
Holy Spirit,

42   and cried out,
> 'Blessed are you among women,
> and blessed is your child!

43   What an honour it is to have the mother of my Lord
> come to see me!

44   As soon as your greeting reached my ears,
> the child within me jumped for joy!

45   Oh, how happy is the woman who believes in God,
> for his promises to her come true.'

46   Then Elisabeth said,
> 'My heart is overflowing with praise of my Lord,

47   my soul is full of joy in God my Saviour.

48   For he has deigned to notice me, his humble servant
> and all generations to come
> will call me the happiest of women!

49   The One who can do all things
> has done great things for me –
> oh, holy is his Name!

50   Truly, his mercy rests on those who fear him
> in every generation.

51   He has shown the strength of his arm,
> he has swept away the high and mighty.

52   He has set kings down from their thrones
      and lifted up the humble.
53   He has satisfied the hungry with good things
      and sent the rich away with empty hands.
54   Yes, he has helped Israel, his child:
55   he has remembered the mercy
      that he promised to our forefathers,
      to Abraham and his sons for evermore!'
56   So Mary stayed with Elisabeth about three months,
      and then went back to her own home.

Luke has set up the two 'panels' of his diptych, his two themes of the parents of John and the parents of Jesus. Now he brings the two together before parting them again for the separate birth stories. This is a skilful way of enriching the interest of the narrative, very like the way a composer of music binds together two themes which he has announced before. Theologically it is an opportunity to make quite clear the relative importance of the two children who are to be born (Elisabeth's speech, verses 41–45). It also provides a point of resolution and rest at which the theology, the underlying ideas, can come out into the open: Elisabeth's song of praise in verses 46–55. This was a device which the historians of the time and the writers of the Old Testament particularly liked – a break in the action which enables one of the chief characters to utter a monologue explaining what has been going on. If there were any sources, they could be used. If not, it was perfectly in order for the writer to use his own resources in an appropriate way. Matthew and John in their gospels used this convention at length. Luke is more sparing because he does not like to leave his narrative out in the cold too long, but he uses it just as effectively.

The speeches of both Elisabeth and Mary in this passage are in the form of poetry. The models for Hebrew poetry are the Psalms. Like some modern verse (e.g. T. S. Eliot's) they are not shaped by rhymes but by a loose sustaining rhythm. Particularly Jewish is the way one half of a verse balances the other: *My heart is overflowing with praise of my Lord/my soul is full of joy in God my Saviour*. There one half repeats the other in different words, but they can contrast: *He has satisfied the hungry with good things/and sent the rich away with empty hands*. The Dead Sea Scrolls have shown us that the composition of such psalms was going on in Jewish circles just before the time of the gospels. Further instances in St Paul's letters and Revelation show that the Christians took up the form and used it as Luke has done, particularly happily, in his three famous canticles.

The only dramatic incident in this passage is John's stirring inside his mother's womb, a common feature of pregnancy which is used here to show the agitation of the unborn child at the presence of his Lord – like Zacharias' or Mary's agitation when faced by Gabriel. Elisabeth's being *filled with the Holy Spirit* means that the words she is about to speak are true theology, inspired by God. Her praise of Mary and her child has been taken up in the popular devotion of the Catholic church, which has unfortunately made Protestants (however biblical) shy of it. The theme of God's irrevocable and effective word, and the blessed fulfilment of a trusting response to it, is resumed in verse 45.

Elisabeth's[3] song is rich with the Old Testament references and reminiscences of which Luke is so fond, for they show the continuity of the old order with the new. It is the same God who governs both. Hannah's song in 1 Samuel 2.1–10 and Psalm 113 are major sources which should not be missed. A well annotated Bible will provide the rest – so many of them that the Magnificat is in fact a smoothly articulated collage of old texts and reminiscences.

3. I have preferred the variant reading of the Latin texts, though many manuscripts have 'Mary' instead. See the footnote in the New English Bible.

The determining element in the theology of Elisabeth's song is the God who comforts and strikes, lifting up the least and the lost, beating down the great and the secure. It is a revolutionary song for a revolutionary religion, founded in the being and doing of a God who up-ends human contrivances. Yet it is confident and happy, for God is tender as well as strong. Verses 44 and 45 clinch the matter. All this is *now*. All the generations from old father Abraham gather towards this point in time, this ordinary woman and her unborn child in the hillside town; and from this point they stream away into eternity. History is illuminated at this little point in the present. From it we see what the past is all about and are shown the direction of the future.

The note of time means that Mary leaves just before Elisabeth's nine months' pregnancy is up, six months before her own delivery is due. It brings us back to earth and back to the story after the ecstatic timelessness of the song.

1. 57–80

57 Then came the time for Elisabeth's child to be born, and she gave birth to a son.

58 Her neighbours and relations heard of the great mercy the Lord had shown her and shared her joy.

59 When the eighth day came, they were going to circumcise the child and call him Zacharias, after his father,

60 but his mother said:
'Oh no! He must be called John.'

61 'But none of your relations is called John,' they replied.

62 And they made signs to his father to see what name he wanted the child to have.

63 He beckoned for a writing-tablet and wrote the words, 'His name is John', which greatly surprised everybody.

64 Then his power of speech quite suddenly came back, and his first words were to thank God.

65 The neighbours were awe-struck at this, and all these incidents were reported in the hill-country of Judaea.

66 People turned the whole matter over in their hearts, and said,

'What is this child's future going to be? For the Lord's blessing is plainly upon him.'

67 Then Zacharias, his father, filled with the Holy Spirit and speaking like a prophet, said,

68 'Blessings on the Lord, the God of Israel,
because he has turned his face towards his people
and has set them free!

69 And he has raised up for us a standard of salvation
in the house of his servant David.

70 Long, long ago, through the words of his holy
prophets,
he promised to do this for us,

71 so that we should be safe from our enemies
and secure from all who hate us.

72 So does he continue the mercy
he showed to our forefathers.
So does he remember the holy agreement
he made with them

73 and the oath which he swore to our father Abraham,

74 to make us this gift:
that we should be saved
from the hands of our enemies,
and in his presence should serve him unafraid

75 in holiness and righteousness all our lives.

76 'And you, little child, will be called the prophet
of the Most High;
for you will go before the Lord
to prepare the way for his coming.

77 It will be for you to give his people
knowledge of their salvation
through the forgiveness of their sins.

78   Because the heart of our God
        is full of mercy towards us,
        the first light of Heaven shall come to visit us –
79   to shine on those who lie in darkness and under the
            shadow of death,
        and to guide our feet into the path of peace.'
80   The little child grew up and became strong in spirit.
        He lived in lonely places until the day came for him to
        show himself to Israel.

After the conjunction of the two stories in the previous passage, Luke resumes the first one, John the Baptist's. In this story of his birth two contrasting elements are put together in a way which has theological point. First we see the usual celebration and quarrelling amongst friends and neighbours which attend a big family event. Then we hear a great hymn in praise of God's faithfulness and mercy. It is odd, but very Lucan, that these two worlds of pettiness and glory should belong together.

The Jews traced the ceremony of circumcision back to Abraham as father of their race. There, as always, ritual links the new birth to the age-old world of tradition and the remote past. But when it comes to the question of the boy's name and the heated argument over it, then it emerges that something quite new has happened. It was usual for a boy to be called after his father, and names were more important then than now. A name showed who a man was and where he came from. The new name of John, previously unheard in this family, marks and signifies a new beginning. It points to the fact that John belongs elsewhere than in the family circle. When Zacharias resolves the argument by obeying Gabriel's command (1.13) his punishment of dumbness is taken away because he is at last co-operating with God's will. *The neighbours were awe-struck* – the usual and appropriate reaction to God's doings in this gospel. Verses 66 and

67 form a bridge passage from the domestic to the theological-poetic scene.

As with Elisabeth at verse 41 it is noted that Zacharias speaks in the Spirit. There was no need to say this of Mary before her song, for the Spirit abides with her because of her son. It prepares the reader for the kind of inspired and exalted utterance which formed a usual part of the worship of the early church. As with Elisabeth's song, Zacharias' is so full of Old Testament quotation and reference as almost to be made of it. Inspired scripture suits an inspired song and lends it the resonance and dignity which only old words and phrases can give.

The song is about God in history. It celebrates the end of three centuries of waiting and anxiety, the return of God to his people whom he had seemed to have forgotten. As in Mary's song, a long historical perspective from Abraham through David comes to resolution in the present. The hopes for deliverance and comfort in the Psalms, for truth, light and a road to God in the prophets, all these flood back into the light of their realization. Since Abraham figures by name both here and in Elisabeth's song, it is worth remembering the particular importance which the early Christians attached to him as a man of faith who patiently trusted God's word and waited for its fulfilment in the future. For the Christians that future is now. They know what Abraham looked forward to, and Abraham comes home in Christ. They feel like the child waking up on his birthday after counting the days towards it for so long – 'But tomorrow is today!' (See Romans 4, Hebrews 11.8–10.) Verses 76 and 77 describe the part John will play in the salvation which is beginning. *You will go before the Lord* (which could mean Jesus or God or both – Jesus is often 'Lord' in this gospel) *to prepare the way*.

Verse 80 shows Luke's particular interest in growth and development. The second half of the verse carefully puts John out of the picture. We shall not see him again until he takes up his public work at 3.2, so we are finished with the diptych and the way is clear for Luke to tell the story of Jesus' birth and childhood without digression.

2.1–7

1   At that time a proclamation was made by Caesar Augustus that all the inhabited world should be registered.

2   This was the first census, undertaken while Cyrenius was governor of Syria;

3   and everybody went to the town of his birth to be registered.

4   Joseph went up from the town of Nazareth in Galilee to David's town, Bethlehem, in Judaea, because he was a direct descendant of David,

5   to be registered with his future wife, Mary, who was pregnant.

6   So it happened that it was while they were there in Bethlehem that she came to the end of her time.

7   She gave birth to her first child, a son. And as there was no place for them inside the inn, she wrapped him up and laid him in a manger.

The Jewish historian Josephus tells us that Quirinius' census was in A.D. 6–7. He may have been in Palestine earlier than that, but this does suggest that Luke's dating is not accurate. In any case, pin-point precision was not his first concern. Rather, he is making one of his many links; not with the Jewish past this time but with the wider sweep of Gentile history. Very likely he sees Caesar as promoting the purposes of God by bringing Jesus to David's town to be born. Isaiah 2 had seen the Gentile king Cyrus in a similar light because of his hand in bringing about the nation's homecoming. The effect of verses 1–6 is first to fasten and

confirm the Messiahship of Jesus by strengthening his connection with David, secondly to fix his life at the outset in
the context of the whole of human history – *all the inhabited
world*. Verse 7 brings back the theme of the 'fringe'. Jesus is
born on the edge of our busy and comfortable world which
has *no place* for him and in the end pushed him out. Perhaps
there is a reminiscence here of the birth of Moses (Exodus
2.3) which was also in an emergency situation.

2.8–20

8   There were some shepherds living in the same part
of the country, keeping guard throughout the night
over their flock in the open fields.

9   Suddenly an angel of the Lord stood before them, the
splendour of the Lord blazed around them, and they
were terror-stricken.

10 But the angel said to them,
   'Do not be afraid! Listen, I bring you glorious news of
great joy which is for all the people.

11 This very day, in David's town, a Saviour has been born
for you. He is Christ, the Lord.

12 Let this prove it to you: you will find a baby, wrapped up
and lying in a manger.'

13   And in a flash there appeared with the angel a vast host
of the armies of Heaven, praising God, saying,

14   'Glory to God in the highest Heaven! Peace upon
earth among men of goodwill!'

15   When the angels left them and went back into Heaven,
the shepherds said to each other,
   'Now let us go straight to Bethlehem and see this
thing which the Lord has made known to us.'

16   So they went as fast as they could and they found
Mary and Joseph – and the baby lying in the manger.

17 And when they had seen this sight, they told everybody

what had been said to them about the little child.

18 And all those who heard them were amazed at what the shepherds said.

19 But Mary treasured all these things and turned them over in her mind.

20 The shepherds went back to work, glorifying and praising God for everything that they had heard and seen, which had happened just as they had been told.

The theme of this passage is the same as in 1.26–38 (The Annunciation to Mary). Heaven and earth are opened to one another and talk together. But this time it is not a promise: it is the proclamation of its fulfilment. It has happened.

The shepherd's job had both disreputable and glamorous associations. Their work out on the *open fields* and hillsides kept them on the edge of civilized life – including religious life. The rabbis regarded them with suspicion. Their job prevented their being regular church-goers. At the same time it had its dignity and its theology. King David had been a shepherd, so had Moses when God appeared to him (Exodus 3.2), and God himself was the shepherd of his people (Psalm 23). Shepherds belonged to God's poor people, in whom Luke has a particular interest.

Whereas for John *the night* is a symbol of evil, for Luke it brings wonder and a sense of the presence of God. According to him it was the time when Jesus usually prayed, the time of his birth and his transfiguration. This story realizes the promise that God will *shine on those who lie in darkness*.

The word *suddenly* brings back the theme of God's irruption into his world which arouses *terror*. But the shepherds are told *Do not be afraid* because God's presence is not taking the form of an earth-shaking firework-display but of something small, vulnerable and entirely human: *You will find a baby, wrapped up and lying in a manger*.

The *vast host of the armies of Heaven* are God's courtiers. The birth

which has happened *this very day* is *glorious news of great joy*, not
just for the Jews, not just for *all the people*, but for the whole
universe, and that is its setting. The chorus *Glory to God* spans
Heaven and earth. In contrast with the vast scope of all this,
but bound firmly to it, is the ordinary little sight which the
shepherds go to see: *Mary and Joseph – and the baby lying in the
manger*. Their reaction to it is to go *back to work* (as we all have
to), but to do so *glorifying and praising God for everything that they
had heard and seen*. *Glorifying* is Luke's usual word for the happy
state of praise of people who have recognized God's goodwill
and kindness towards them.

Verses 18 and 19 contrast the amazement of the people who
heard the shepherds' tale with the calm way in which *Mary
treasured all these things and turned them over in her mind*. She has got
beyond her initial astonishment and begins to see the meaning and tendency of what has happened. In this way she is an
example both to the evangelist and the reader. These verses
are also an instance of Luke's particular and characteristic
interest in what goes on in people's minds.

2.21–39

21   At the end of the eight days, the time came for circum-
      cising the child and he was called Jesus, the name given
      to him by the angel before his conception.
22   When the 'purification' time, stipulated by the Law of
      Moses, was completed, they brought Jesus to Jerusalem
      to present him to the Lord. –
23   This was to fulfil a requirement of the Lord –
        'Every male that openeth the womb shall be called
      holy to the Lord.'
24   They also offered the sacrifice prescribed by the Law –
        'A pair of turtle doves, or two young pigeons.'
25   In Jerusalem there was at this time a man by the name
      of Simeon. He was an upright man, devoted to the service

of God, living in expectation of the Restoration of Israel. His heart was open to the Holy Spirit,

26 and it had been revealed to him that he would not die before he saw the Lord's Christ.

27 He had been led by the Spirit to go into the Temple, and when Jesus' parents brought the child in to have done to him what the Law required,

28 he took him up in his arms, blessed God and said –

29   'Now, Lord, you are dismissing your servant
    in peace, as you promised!

30   For with my own eyes I have seen your salvation

31   which you have made ready for all peoples to see

32   – a light to show truth to the gentiles
    and bring glory to your people Israel.'

33   The child's father and mother were still amazed at what was said about him,

34 when Simeon gave them his blessing. He said to Mary, the child's mother,

    'This child is destined to make many fall and many rise in Israel and to set up a standard which many will attack –

35 for he will expose the secret thoughts of many hearts. And for you . . . your very soul will be pierced by a sword.'

36   There was also present, Anna, the daughter of Phanuel of the tribe of Asher, who was a prophetess. She was a very old woman, having had seven years' married life

37 and was now a widow of eighty-four. She spent her whole life in the Temple and worshipped God night and day with fastings and prayers.

38 She came up at this very moment, praised God and spoke about Jesus to all those in Jerusalem who were expecting redemption.

39   When they had completed all the requirements of the Law of the Lord, they returned to Galilee to their own

town Nazareth. The child grew up and became strong
and full of wisdom.
40 And God's blessing was upon him.

There is no quarrelling at Jesus' circumcision as there was
at John's. He is called by *the name given to him by the angel before
his conception*, a reminder that God knew him and had a
purpose for him before his birth. Luke's insistence on the
completing of time in verses 22 and 23 is a reversion to a
favourite theme of his and an introduction to his dramatic
portrayal of fulfilment in the characters of Simeon and Anna.
Along with this is the fulfilment of the ceremonies of the Law:
verse 23 has a quotation from Exodus 13.12 which fixes the
origin of this ceremony in the birth of the nation. Verse 24
quotes Leviticus 12 which lays down the sacrifice which
parents should offer for their first son.

To comply with this custom Mary and Joseph must go up
to Jerusalem and the Temple. Previously in this gospel we
have seen only John's father in the Holy City. Jesus' coming
to this centre of God's world forms a long-awaited resolution
in Luke's narrative. Simeon is an embodiment of the old
religion at its best, *living in expectation of the Restoration* (or comforting) *of Israel*. In the *Holy Spirit* and what the Spirit had
revealed to him he already has what had been expected for so
long, as in Joel's prophecy (2.28): 'the day shall come when I
will pour out my spirit on all mankind; your sons and your
daughters shall prophesy, your old men shall dream dreams.'
We must wait until Pentecost for the full coming of the
Spirit to men. Here we have its first fruits.

Simeon's song is the last of Luke's psalms providing, like
the others, an opportunity for the doctrine behind the
events to be uncovered. Again there is the resolution of the
past, Israel's and Simeon's, and the reopening of the future
with a glimpse of the gift of *truth to the gentiles* which will come
about in Acts and which Luke has hinted at by the dating

at the beginning of this chapter. The tranquillity and white hopes of the Nunc Dimittis are balanced by the dark forebodings of Simeon's prophecy in verses 34 and 35. *Falling and rising* is an echo of Mary's song. In the presence of God all that is arrogant and secure is broken down, all that is low and expectant is raised up. Men meet the judgment and the mercy, for God is the one who *will expose the secret thoughts*. The prophecy ends with the first intimation of opposition and suffering in the gospel, a little threatening cloud in the calm skies of the first two chapters.

Anna is little more than a female counterpart of Simeon. Luke has a particular care for women so is glad to introduce the old Jewess at this high point of the story. She recalls the great women of Jewish history like Miriam and Esther. To be a widow meant belonging to an underprivileged and vulnerable class, to be a prophetess meant honour in the sight of God. Such figures were familiar in the church of Luke's time (1 Timothy 5.3–10), and any of them hearing this passage would be able to identify with Anna.

The passage ends with a typical note of continuity and growth (cf. 1.80). *Wisdom* was a gift prized by philosophical Gentiles and devout Jews alike, so precious to Luke.

2.41–52

41 Every year at the Passover festival, Jesus' parents used to go to Jerusalem.
42 When he was twelve years old they went up to the city as usual for the festival.
43 When it was over they started back home, but the boy Jesus stayed behind in Jerusalem, without his parents' knowledge.
44 They went a day's journey assuming that he was somewhere in their company, and then they began to look for him among their relations and acquaintances.

45 They failed to find him, however, and turned back to the
    city, looking for him as they went.

46 Three days later they found him – in the Temple, sitting
    among the teachers, listening to them and asking them
    questions.

47 All those who heard him were astonished at his powers
    of comprehension and at the answers that he gave.

48 When Joseph and Mary saw him, they could hardly
    believe their eyes, and his mother said to him,

    'Why have you treated us like this, my son? Here
    have your father and I been worried, looking for you
    everywhere!'

49 And Jesus replied,

    'But why were you looking for me? Did you not know
    that I must be in my Father's house?'

50 But they did not understand his reply.

51 Then he went home to Nazareth with them and was
    obedient to them. And his mother treasured all these
    things in her heart.

52 And as Jesus continued to grow in body and mind, he
    grew also in the love of God and of those who knew him.

Ancient customs, traditional piety, the significance of
Jerusalem – all these are familiar motifs by now. The Passover
is particularly appropriate for this last story because it is a
ceremony for the whole nation simultaneously (previous
rituals have been family occasions), and because it celebrates
Israel's salvation in the past and looks towards it in the future.
Jesus is now *twelve years old*, which means that he has reached
the age of responsibility and is 'a son of the law'. His maturity
– either precocious or supernatural – is seen in the contrast
of his calm authority with his parents' anxiety and fuss. He
has his own destiny which they *did not understand* – a common
enough feature of adolescence, but here also a dramatic
development of the doctrine of his divine sonship. *Did you not*

know that I must be in my Father's house? Yet at the end *he went home ...
with them and was obedient to them.* The real break is to come later
at 8.19. Now it is simply made clear that he has a setting other
than his family.

We are in a transitional phase of Luke's narrative as of
Jesus' life – a bridge passage. His relations with his parents
bring that out. Jesus' conversation with the teachers tells of
a more far-reaching transition. His *listening* witnesses to his
reverence for the old teaching – an exemplary Jewish boy.
Yet his position at the centre is an image of something more
than that, a hint that he is what the old doctrines are all
about. Verse 46 *(Three days later, they found him)* very likely points
towards the resurrection when he was restored to his people
after three days' lost.

The passage ends with a last glimpse of Mary as an example
of meditation for the reader, and a typical note of development which sets Jesus in the divine and human context of
love.

3

The Desert – The Dawn Wind Rises

3. 1–6

1 In the fifteenth year of the reign of the Emperor Tiberius (a year when Pontius Pilate was governor of Judaea, Herod tetrarch of Galilee, Philip, his brother, tetrarch of the territory of Ituraea and Trachonitis, and Lysanias tetrarch of Abilene,

2 while Annas and Caiaphas were the High Priests), the word of God came to John, the son of Zacharias, while he was in the desert.

3 He went into the whole country round about the Jordan proclaiming baptism as a mark of a complete change of heart and of the forgiveness of sins,

4 as the book of the prophet Isaiah says –
   The voice of one crying in the wilderness,
   Make ye ready the way of the Lord,
   Make his paths straight.

5 Every valley shall be filled,
   And every mountain and hill shall be brought low:
   And the crooked shall become straight,
   And the rough ways smooth:

6 And all flesh shall see the salvation of God.

The scene shifts from private to public life. Luke marks the change with a sonorous new beginning. Again the dating is not entirely precise – some time between A.D. 27 and 29. The first two verses do two things: the great list of rulers has the effect of a ceremonious opening or fanfare and it fixes the story in the civilized, secular world more firmly and fully than 2.1. It gathers to a climax with *The word of God came to John, the son of Zacharias*, echoing Jeremiah 1.2. The *desert* is the setting of the Exodus, the place where God was near to his people, comforting and testing them. That was why it had a pull on the mind of serious Jews like the Dead Sea sect. Jordan is the gateway to the promised land.

The grand opening and the desert/Jordan scene thus promise some new experience of God. Verses 3 to 6 describe how it begins: *a complete change of heart* and the *forgiveness of sins* which cut away the hold of the guilty and muddled past. This comes about by means of baptism. The origins of this rite are obscure, if rich in symbolism. According to some it was the way by which outsiders became Jews, so that when Jews underwent it they put themselves in the position of outsiders and then became people of God afresh. Luke adds a further two verses to the quotation from Isaiah used by Mark and Matthew. Verse 5 brings back the theology of Elisabeth's song: God as the upsetter of our familiar world. Verse 6 echoes Simeon's song and clinches its vision of universal salvation, opening a wider context than Mark and Matthew did at this point. Luke leaves out their description of John's appearance and diet because they make him look like Elijah: a resemblance which Luke wishes to keep for Jesus as well as John (see 7.11–17).

3.7–20

7 So John used to say to the crowds who came out to be baptized by him,

  'Who warned you, you serpent's brood, to escape from the wrath to come?

8 See that your lives prove that your hearts are really changed! Don't start thinking that you can say to yourselves, "We are Abraham's children", for I tell you that God could produce children of Abraham out of these stones!

9　The axe already lies at the root of the tree, and the tree
that fails to produce good fruit is cut down and thrown
into the fire.'

10　Then the crowds would ask him, 'Then what shall
we do?'

11　And his answer was, 'The man who has two shirts
must share with the man who has none, and the man
who has food must do the same.'

12　Some of the tax-collectors also came to him to be
baptized and they asked him,
'Master, what are we to do?'

13　'You must not demand more than you are entitled
to,' he replied.

14　And the soldiers asked him, 'And what are we to do?'
'Don't bully people, don't bring false charges, and be
content with your pay,' he replied.

15　The people were in a great state of expectation and
were all inwardly debating whether John could possibly
be Christ.

16　But John answered them all in these words,
'It is true that I baptize you with water, but the one
who follows me is stronger than I am – indeed I am not
fit to undo his shoe-laces – he will baptize you with the
fire of the Holy Spirit.

17　He will come all ready to separate the wheat from the
chaff, and to clear the rubbish from his threshing-floor.
The wheat he will gather into his barn and the chaff he
will burn with a fire that cannot be put out.'

18　These and many other things John said to the people
as he exhorted them and announced the good news.

19　But the tetrarch Herod, who had been condemned by
John in the affair of Herodias, his brother's wife, as well
as for the other evil things that he had done,

20　crowned his misdeeds by putting John in prison.

Tension mounts as the time of salvation gets nearer. Every life is put under the pressure of the demand for reform. Then John points to the *stronger* one who is to follow him. With verse 17 his message reaches a crackling and menacing climax, after which he disappears from the scene and the story.

Verses 7–9 are material which is found in Matthew too. They are levelled at the Jews, Abraham's children. Their national and religious status will not protect them against the things that are about to happen. God is not bound by these distinctions. He has the power to bring new life where there was none before, and on the other side of this creativity there is judgment – the axe is laid to the root of the tree. This is Luke's constant theology: raising up and throwing down. In verses 10–14 Luke extends John's message and increases its scope with material of his own. Where Matthew has John preaching to the Pharisees and Sadducees, Luke has *the crowds*. Then the word reaches out to the suspect fringes of Jewry, *the tax-collectors*. Last, it is spoken to *the soldiers* who are no doubt Gentiles in the Roman army. The widening pattern is typical of Luke.

John's preaching is stern and inspired enough for people to think of him as the Messiah. So he points away from himself and promises one who will bring an even more searching judgment and fuller inspiration. The symbol of *fire* conveys both life and destruction. The *Holy Spirit* is the long awaited presence of God, dynamic and creative. It is like the wind at harvest home which serves to blow away the light *chaff* from the *threshing floor* and leave only the heavier *wheat* (compare the strong driving wind at Pentecost, Acts 2.2).

With this proclamation of the rising storm and the mounting fire John disappears – a superb exit line. The information about his imprisonment comes from Mark 6.17–18.

3.21–38

21 When all the people had been baptized, and Jesus was praying after his own baptism, Heaven opened

22 and the Holy Spirit came down upon him in the bodily form of a dove. Then there came a voice from Heaven, saying,

'You are my dearly-loved Son, in whom I am well pleased.'

23 Jesus himself was about thirty years old at this time when he began his work.

People assumed that Jesus was the son of Joseph, who was the son of Heli,

24 who was the son of Matthat, who was the son of Levi, who was the son of Melchi, who was the son of Jannai, who was the son of Joseph,

25 who was the son of Mattathias, who was the son of Amos, who was the son of Nahum, who was the son of Esli, who was the son of Naggai,

26 who was the son of Maath, who was the son of Mattathias, who was the son of Semein, who was the son of Josech, who was the son of Joda,

27 who was the son of Joanan, who was the son of Rhesa, who was the son of Zerubbabel, who was the son of Shealtiel, who was the son of Neri,

28 who was the son of Melchi, who was the son of Addi, who was the son of Cosam, who was the son of Elmadam, who was the son of Er,

29 who was the son of Jesus, who was the son of Eliezer, who was the son of Jorim, who was the son of Matthat, who was the son of Levi,

30 who was the son of Symeon, who was the son of Judas, who was the son of Joseph, who was the son of Jonam, who was the son of Eliakim,

31 who was the son of Melea, who was the son of Menna,

who was the son of Mattatha, who was the son of
Nathan, who was the son of David,

32 who was the son of Jesse, who was the son of Obed, who
was the son of Boaz, who was the son of Salmon, who
was the son of Nahshon,

33 who was the son of Amminadab, who was the son of
Arni, who was the son of Hezron, who was the son of
Perez, who was the son of Judah,

34 who was the son of Jacob, who was the son of Isaac, who
was the son of Abraham, who was the son of Terah, who
was the son of Nahor,

35 who was the son of Serug, who was the son of Reu, who
was the son of Peleg, who was the son of Eber, who was
the son of Shelah,

36 who was the son of Cainan, who was the son of
Arphaxad, who was the son of Shem, who was the son
of Noah, who was the son of Lamech,

37 who was the son of Methuselah, who was the son of
Enoch, who was the son of Jared, who was the son of
Mahalaleel, who was the son of Cainan,

38 who was the son of Enos, who was the son of Seth, who
was the son of Adam, who was the son of God.

Luke's eagerness to get John off the stage at a point of
climax and leave it clear for Jesus means that we have no
scene of Jesus' baptism by John as in Matthew and Mark; so
the things which happened then in those gospels are here
transposed to *after his own baptism* when he *was praying*. Luke is
particularly interested in Jesus as a man of prayer (cf. 5.16,
6.12, 9.18 and 28, 11.1 which are all peculiar to Luke). In this
detail as well as his re-arrangement of the traditional material
in the interests of clearer theology and tidier narrative, Luke
shows his hand.

‘ As in the other two gospels this is the opportunity for a
grand symbolic tableau which makes it clear who Jesus is.

Luke's *When all the people had been baptized* sets Jesus among the
rest of the Jewish community – and yet apart. *Praying* is the
point at which earth is opened up to Heaven, and Heaven to
earth. It is easy for Luke to say *Heaven opened* because, like
everybody else in those days, he thought of the sky as something solid (the 'firmament' of Genesis 1), a 'great inverted
bowl' cutting off the dwelling-place of God and his angels
from the world of men. The opening of Heaven thus means
that God and man are accessible to one another through
Jesus, that they meet at the point of Jesus. The angelic
visitations earlier in the story are 'capped' by this, just as the
earlier inspirations of the *Holy Spirit* (Zacharias, Mary, Simeon)
are defined and transcended when it comes *down upon him*.
The *dove* probably echoes Genesis 1.2 or Noah's 'sweet mes-
senger of rest' of Genesis 8.12. On both occasions a new world
is about to begin. The *bodily form* is Lucan realism – not at its
best (cf. 24.36–43). The *voice from Heaven* makes it all clear. In
the old words of scripture (Psalm 2 and Isaiah 42) God speaks
his new word which consists in saying that Jesus is his – *his
dearly-loved son* and his joy. The long waiting is fulfilled, not
just by a word, but by a human presence.

A typical note of time brings the story down from the
sublime and symbolic to the level of history.

Modern readers are likely to skip the genealogy. It is
obscure but not without point or interest. Readers of the
Old Testament will know that this is a familiar biblical form.
Luke's use of it shows his familiarity with the scriptures and
his reverence for them. This is one of many points where the
Jewishness of this gospel stands out, contradicting the old
view that it is a Gentile work. The main concern is to show
Jesus as the Son of God, which links it to the preceding
baptism story and the temptation which follows it. Whereas
those two sections are dramatic, this genealogy is far from it.
But it does give an account of Jesus' divine sonship in terms
of previous history. The title Son of God is given an historical

perspective and continuity with the Old Testament. This is why the genealogy works backwards, and why it goes back beyond Abraham (contrast Matthew) to Adam (father of all men) and God (creator of all). It is, in fact, a particularly good example of Luke's ability to press old forms into the service of new realities. Just as the baptism scene had shown Jesus as Son of God vertically by divine fiat, so the genealogy shows his sonship horizontally by connections in the line of human generation.

4. 1–13

1 Jesus returned from the Jordan full of the Holy Spirit and he was led by the Spirit

2 to spend forty days in the desert, where he was tempted by the devil. He ate nothing during that time and afterwards he felt very hungry.

3 'If you are the Son of God,' the devil said to him, 'tell this stone to turn into a loaf.'

4 Jesus answered,
   'The scripture says, "Man shall not live by bread alone." '

5 Then the devil took him up and showed him all the kingdoms of mankind in a sudden vision,

6 and said to him,
   'I will give you all this power and magnificence, for it belongs to me and I can give it to anyone I please.

7 It shall all be yours if you will fall down and worship me.'

8 To this Jesus replied,
   'It is written, "Thou shalt worship the Lord thy God and him only shalt thou serve." '

9 Then the devil took him to Jerusalem and set him on the highest pinnacle of the Temple.
   'If you are the Son of God,' he said, 'throw yourself down from here,

10 for the scripture says, "He shall give his angels charge concerning thee, to guard thee,"

11 and "On their hands they shall bear thee up, lest haply thou dash thy foot against a stone." '

12 To which Jesus replied,
'It is also said, "Thou shalt not tempt the Lord thy God." '

13 And when he had exhausted every kind of temptation, the devil withdrew until his next opportunity.

The testing of the hero is a favourite theme in folk and fairy tales. There are biblical examples in the stories of Adam, Job, Joseph, Daniel, etc. As well as being exciting, such tales have the deeper value of showing (dramatically) the stuff the hero is made of by describing his reaction to the testing which comes to everybody in some way, but to the hero in a particularly sharp and concentrated form.

The presence of the devil as a character in the drama is a strong indication that we are in the region of fairy tale where there are no abstractions like 'evil' but only evil beings – and the devil is *the* evil being. He is in modern terms a characterization of an internal force, embodying whatever it is that cuts us off from a full and happy life – i.e. from God. Edwin Muir's poem 'The Intercepter' (*Collected Poems*, p. 180), and William Blake's 'To the Accuser who is The God of this World', will be far more use to the reader than any commentary's remarks. In biblical imagery the devil is the one who seeks to prise apart, by whatever means, the trusting relationship of God and man. Jesus, God's man, is therefore a key target for him, but his activities only reveal the unbreakable obedience of Jesus' dependence on God. The devil can never be beaten by those who oppose him with their own resources, only by those who go over his head to his acknowledged superior, and appeal to God. Like any other bureaucrat he cannot abide this treatment. Jesus' constant appeal to the sovereign freedom of God baffles him. Luke can therefore remove him from the scene at verse 13. But he is not rid of him. At the *next opportunity* (literally, at an opportune time) he will be back. Luke is thinking of the final trial and conflict in Jerusalem at the end of his book.

Jesus does not answer the devil out of his own resources but by an appeal to the supremacy of God. Neither does he answer in his own words but in texts from scripture, each of which refers to the failure of Israel to resist similar temptations in the past. So Jesus is shown as the starting-point for a new and truer community of God's people, centred more on God than on their own existence.

Man shall not live by bread alone refers to Deuteronomy 8.3 which recalls the Israelites' impatient crying for bread in the wilderness.

Thou shalt worship the Lord thy God and him only shalt thou serve is from Deuteronomy 6.13 with memories of the false worship of Aaron's golden calf.

Thou shalt not tempt the Lord thy God is Deuteronomy 6.16 and recollects the way in which the Israelites were for ever probing and testing God, seeing if they could get him to work for them in spectacular and reassuring ways.

Luke's narrative is the same as Matthew's except for two important changes. The latter part of verse 6 (. . . *power and magnificence, for it belongs to me and I can give it to anyone I please*) is added by Luke, the most secular and ascetic of gospel-writers. True, the world is the Lord's, but the enemy has a foothold in it, and particularly in the power and magnificence (cf. 22.25 and 26). Luke is aware of the temptations of his cultivated and influential readers. The second change of Luke's is to end with the Temple parapet story instead of the kingdoms of the world like Matthew. He adds *to Jerusalem*, so very likely he is making a familiar pattern with Jerusalem as a climax (cf. the birth stories and, more important, the shape of the gospel as a whole).

Galilee – The Morning of the Kingdom

4.14–30

14 And now Jesus returned to Galilee in the power of the Spirit, and news of him spread through all the surrounding district.

15 He taught in their synagogues, to everyone's great admiration.

16 Then he came to Nazareth where he had been brought up and, according to his custom, went to the synagogue on the Sabbath day. He stood up to read the scriptures

17 and the book of the prophet Isaiah was handed to him. He opened the book and found the place where these words are written –

18   The Spirit of the Lord is upon me,
    Because he anointed me to preach good tidings to
       the poor:
    He hath sent me to proclaim release to the captives,
    And recovering of sight to the blind,
    To set at liberty them that are bruised,

19   To proclaim the acceptable year of the Lord.

20 Then he shut the book, handed it back to the attendant and resumed his seat. Every eye in the synagogue was fixed upon him

21 and he began to tell them, 'This very day this scripture has been fulfilled, while you have been listening to it!'

22 Everybody heard what he said. They were amazed at the beautiful words that came from his lips, and they kept saying,

    'Isn't this Joseph's son?'

23 So he said to them,
    'I expect you will quote this proverb to me, "Cure
    yourself, doctor!" Let us see you do in your own country
    all that we have heard that you did in Capernaum!'
24 Then he added, 'I assure you that no prophet is ever
    welcomed in his own country.
25 I tell you the plain fact that in Elijah's time, when the
    heavens were shut up for three and a half years and there
    was a great famine through the whole country, there
    were many widows of Israel,
26 but Elijah was not sent to any of them. But he *was* sent
    to Sarepta, to a widow in the country of Sidon.
27 In the time of Elisha the prophet, there were many lepers
    in Israel, but not one of them was healed – only Naaman,
    the Syrian.'
28 But when they heard this, everyone in the synagogue
    was furiously angry.
29 They sprang to their feet and drove him right out of the
    town, taking him to the brow of the hill on which it
    was built, intending to hurl him down bodily.
30 But he walked straight through the whole crowd and
    went on his way.

The last of the temptations left us in Jerusalem. Now we go
back to Galilee and Nazareth. We shall not be in Jerusalem
again until the end of the gospel. Instead of the frequent
switches from Jerusalem to Galilee which characterized the
early chapters and introduced us to the symbolism of Luke's
geography, we now have a ministry in the towns and villages
of Galilee followed by a long journey to Jerusalem which
begins at 9.51 and reaches its destination at 19.28. These are
not aimless wanderings but *in the power of the Spirit*. They are
the way in which salvation is worked out. Underneath it all
is the symbol of life as a journey which Bunyan used in the
same way as Luke in his *Pilgrim's Progress*.

Synagogues were to be found in towns where there were Jewish communities, even as far away as Corinth and Rome. They were places where the Law (i.e. the Old Testament, not just the first five books of it) was read out and interpreted. They provided a focus for religion other than the Temple and nearer to hand. They were less official than the Temple with its hierarchy, so an ordinary Jew like Jesus could take a leading part in its service. By beginning in a synagogue Luke has Jesus' ministry follow the same strategy as Paul's in Acts.

It is typical of the gospel that its radical newness is expressed by the old scripture of the book of the prophet Isaiah. Only one comment is needed to make it complete: *This very day this scripture has been fulfilled, while you have been listening to it!* There is no more waiting. Tomorrow is today. That is the gospel. And who is the good news for? *The poor, the captives, the blind, the bruised* – for those who know they need it and no one else.

No sooner has it been proclaimed than people start to be upset. Can such *beautiful words*, such a sublime and long-awaited thing, come from this ordinary man whom they know so well: *Isn't this Joseph's son?* Familiarity breeds contempt. The Nazareth of this scene is a more ambiguous place than the quiet and promising home of the first two chapters. The conflict which is to go on all through the story begins here. Jesus' answer to his critics is to upset them even more. In a speech which takes up the theme of God's presence on the fringes of life, puts the weight of Old Testament tradition behind that theme and glimpses the future of the Acts of the Apostles, he appeals to the example of God's prophets Elijah and Elisha who were sent to help outsiders although there was work to do inside Israel. The reaction to this daring fusion of respected traditions and unofficial newness is instant and violent.

The whole passage is very much Luke. The setting and the sayings *Is not this the son of . . .* and *no prophet is ever welcomed in his own country* are all that we can be sure he has got from previous

writers. They come from Mark's gospel. It is likely that Luke
has made this scene to dramatize the second of these sayings.
Beginning with Mark's proverb and report of rejection in a
synagogue, he spins a story out of Old Testament references
and his own narrative skill, with the result that is before us.
But of course Luke is not just telling the tale. Tales are for
him the way to get the truth across, and so he gives us something of great value and dramatic force which is not in the
other gospels: an opening scene which makes very clear both
what the gospel is and why it is going to cause trouble. The
theme will go on right through to the end of Acts: the poor,
the bruised, the outsiders – these are the ones who accept the
good news. But his own people do not want to know about
him to the bitter end (Acts 28. 23–28). The radical newness
and sharp conflict here contrast with the idyllic, traditional
calm of the birth stories.

4.31–44

31   Then he came down to Capernaum, a town in Galilee,
      and taught them on the Sabbath day.

32   They were astonished at his teaching, for his words had
      the ring of authority.

33   There was a man in the synagogue under the influence
      of some evil spirit and he yelled at the top of his voice,

34   'Hi! What have you got to do with us, Jesus, you Nazar-
      ene – have you come to kill us? I know who you are all
      right, you're God's holy one!'

35   Jesus cut him short and spoke sharply,
        'Be quiet! Get out of him!'
      And after throwing the man down in front of them,
      the devil did come out of him without hurting him in
      the slightest.

36   At this everybody present was amazed and they kept
      saying to each other,

'What sort of words are these? He speaks to these evil spirits with authority and power and out they go.'

37 And his reputation spread over the whole surrounding district.

38 When Jesus got up and left the synagogue he went into Simon's house. Simon's mother-in-law was suffering in the grip of a high fever, and they asked Jesus to help her.

39 He stood over her as she lay in bed, brought the fever under control and it left her. At once she got up and began to see to their needs.

40 Then, as the sun was setting, all those who had friends suffering from every kind of disease brought them to Jesus and he laid his hands on each one of them separately and healed them.

41 Evil spirits came out of many of these people, shouting, 'You are the Son of God!'

But he spoke sharply to them and would not allow them to say any more, for they knew perfectly well that he was Christ.

42 At daybreak, he went off to a deserted place, but the crowds tried to find him and when they did discover him, tried to prevent him from leaving them.

43 But he told them, 'I must tell the good news of the kingdom of God to other towns as well – that is my mission.'

44 And he continued proclaiming his message in the synagogues of Judaea.

Luke follows his great opening scene with a string of incidents which he has taken from Mark's gospel, adding only a few touches of his own and abbreviating Mark at some points. As this part of the narrative is episodic and sketchy, comments on it will be episodic and sketchy too. The overall plan is to show the manifesto of 4.18 and 19 working itself out in word and action. Luke has already told us what these episodes mean to him: they *proclaim the accept-*

able year of the Lord, the effect of God's presence among men.

The ring of authority has nothing to do with hierarchies or institutions, but validates itself by the power of what is said and done.

The Bible does not see man as an independent or self-subsisting being. He is open to evil powers which debase him and good powers which exalt him, so madness is explained as being *under the influence of some evil spirit* – the sufferer's body has been invaded by an alien and destructive force. 'We are lived by powers we pretend to understand' (W. H. Auden). The spirit shouts: *I know who you are* because one spiritual force recognizes another instantly, particularly if it is hostile, in the same way as we sense a friendly or unfriendly place or person. Jesus and the evil spirits are on the same plane, but Jesus, *the Son of God*, is stronger and greater than they are – a reality which was clinched by his resurrection which Christians see as his conquest of evil and destructive forces. The (unspoken) answer to the question *What sort of words are these?* is, 'It is the creative word of God, calling men now from their confused and enslaved lives into full life, just as once it called the world into existence out of chaos and Israel from slavery into freedom.'

Simon's mother-in-law's fever is also seen as a demon to be *brought under control*. She shows her return to health by seeing to the needs of others – an example for all Luke's readers.

Why does Jesus stop the evil spirits shouting out who he is? Is it wise to forbid free publicity like this? Luke's own answer could well be that Jesus' identity is only clear when his story is complete. Luke is handling a theme (secrecy) which plays a large part in his source, Mark, where it gives difficulty to the commentators. Its role is much reduced in Luke's version, but no less puzzling: yet a theology without it would be banal and false. The whole object of his work is man's free response, not demonic acclamation.

The last paragraph has a touch of Luke's own hand. Where
Mark, his source, has Simon trying to find him, here it is
the crowds. Luke is particularly aware of the wider setting of
the gospel, and that little dramatic adjustment does it for
him. (Simon doesn't lose out, however, for he has a leading
part in the next story.) The scope of the gospel mission is
indicated in Jesus' reply to the crowds. He must leave them
to go to 'other towns as well'. The concluding sentence
shows Jesus' mission in Judaea being conducted under the
same strategy as Paul's in Asia Minor – synagogue to synagogue.

5. 1–11

1   One day the people were crowding closely round
Jesus to hear God's message, as he stood on the shore of
Lake Gennesaret.

2   Jesus noticed two boats drawn up on the beach, for the
fishermen had left them there while they were cleaning
their nets.

3   He went aboard one of the boats, which belonged to
Simon, and asked him to push out a little from the shore.
Then he sat down and continued his teaching of the
crowds from the boat.

4   When he had finished speaking, he said to Simon,
'Push out now into deep water and let down your nets
for a catch.'

5   Simon replied, 'Master! We've worked all night and
never caught a thing, but if you say so, I'll let the nets
down.'

6   And when they had done this, they caught an enormous shoal of fish – so big that the nets began to tear.

7   So they signalled to their partners in the other boat to
come and help them. They came and filled both the
boats to sinking point.

8   When Simon Peter saw this, he fell at Jesus' knees and said,

'Keep away from me, Lord, for I'm only a sinful man!'

9   For he and his companions

10   (including Zebedee's sons, James and John, Simon's partners) were staggered at the haul of fish they had made.

Jesus said to Simon, 'Don't be afraid, Simon. From now on your catch will be *men*.'

11   So they brought the boats ashore, left everything and followed him.

Another big scene lets us see the architecture of Luke's scheme. In the two previous sections he has set out Jesus' mission in theology and story, as it had been prophesied and prepared for in the opening chapters. Now he makes an important link by again joining on something which will carry on right to the end of Acts – the share of the disciples of Jesus in his work. Mark had this happen immediately after Jesus appeared on the scene. Luke takes more space, and shows a subtler sense of time and the course of history. He keeps it aside until the nature of the gospel mission has been made clearer and fuller than had been done by Mark's single sentence (Mark 1.15), because he wants the reader to know more about the work which the disciples are called to do before joining them on to it. As in the earlier chapters (e.g. Zacharias, the shepherds), God steps in while people are quietly going about their ordinary business – *cleaning their nets* in this case. As with the characters in the early stories, the coming of God's power into their lives frightens them. The reply is the same: *Don't be afraid*, for this power is not going to annihilate the world but remake it.

The story which follows is a sketch for Acts. It is found again in chapter 21 of John's gospel. There it takes place after the resurrection. Two things explain this discrepancy, which may look like carelessness on the part of the gospel-writers. One, that stories about Jesus circulated without any clear note as to when they happened: it was for the writers to string them together. The other, that for the early Christians the risen Jesus, the Jesus they knew in their experience, was the same as the historical man who lived before his crucifixion. We have already had a glimpse of this in the previous passage with Jesus' power over the demons: no doubt it was there in his lifetime, but it was even clearer after it, and Luke lived in that 'after'.

The last line of the story: *Don't be afraid, Simon. From now on your catch will be men* shows the point. The Christian reader can easily identify with Simon's disillusionment and weariness over his work. But the command to him is the same: *Push out now into deep water*, the frightening and unfamiliar places where they have not been before. Luke is the great historian of the church's launching out beyond the home waters of religion and Judaism. This theme of the expanding mission of the church is present in this story and shapes it. Whereas John puts this story after the resurrection, Luke sees it overlapping and linking into the life of Jesus. Just as the gospel frequently works forward to Acts, so Acts will constantly look back to Jesus.

Simon Peter, James and John form a trio which represents the church. We shall meet them again at important moments. Here they are the model disciples who give Jesus' call priority over their own exhaustion and limitations and in the end *left everything and followed him*.

5.12–26

12   While he was in one of the towns, Jesus came upon a man who was a mass of leprosy. When he saw Jesus, he prostrated himself before him and begged,
   'If you want to Lord, you can make me clean.'

13 Jesus stretched out his hand, placed it on the leper, saying,

'Certainly I want to. Be clean!'

Immediately the leprosy left him

14 and Jesus warned him not to tell anybody, but to go and show himself to the priest and to make the offerings for his recovery which Moses prescribed, as evidence to the authorities.

15 Yet the news about him spread all the more, and enormous crowds collected to hear Jesus and to be healed of their complaints.

16 But he slipped quietly away to deserted places for prayer.

17 One day while Jesus was teaching, some Pharisees and experts in the Law were sitting near him. They had come out of every village in Galilee and Judaea as well as from Jerusalem. The Lord's power to heal people was with him.

18 Soon some men arrived carrying a paralytic on a small bed and they kept trying to carry him in to put him down in front of Jesus.

19 When they failed to find a way of getting him in because of the dense crowd, they went up on to the top of the house and let him down, bed and all, through the tiles, into the middle of the crowd in front of Jesus.

20 When Jesus saw their faith, he said to the man,

'My friend, your sins are forgiven.'

21 The scribes and the Pharisees began to argue about this, saying,

'Who is this man who talks blasphemy? Who can forgive sins? Only God can do that.'

22 Jesus realized what was going on in their minds and spoke straight to them.

'Why must you argue like this in your minds?

23 Which do you suppose is easier – to say, "Your sins are forgiven" or to say, "Get up and walk"?

24 But to make you realize that the Son of Man has full
   authority on earth to forgive sins – I tell *you*,' he said to the
   man who was paralysed, 'get up, pick up your bed and
   go home!'
25   Instantly the man sprang to his feet before their eyes,
   picked up the bedding on which he used to lie, and went
   off home, praising God.
26 Sheer amazement gripped every man present, and they
   praised God and said in awed voices, 'We have seen
   incredible things today.'

  Luke now picks up Mark's gospel again at the point where
he had left it for the insertion of the last scene – Mark 1.40.
He will follow Mark continuously up to 6.20 (Mark's 3.19),
so for the next few pages we shall be reading Mark, trimmed
up, edited, and occasionally re-arranged by Luke.
  Lepers were forced to live on the edge of the community
because of their disease. The touch of Jesus' hand breaks the
isolation and the taboo. It is a cure in response to faith:
notice how the leper behaves like a man at worship, pros-
trating himself in front of Jesus, and addressing him as if he
were praying to God, *If you want to Lord, you can make me clean* –
'Lord' being the title by which Christians knew Jesus and
God. Again Jesus does not want sensational publicity and is
careful to work within the old regulations. For the priests'
responsibilities as public health inspectors in cases of leprosy
see Leviticus 13 and 14. *As evidence to the authorities* means evidence that the leper is cured and fit to enter normal society,
not evidence of Jesus' power. To Mark's account of Jesus
escaping into the solitude of the desert Luke adds *for prayer*.
This characteristic touch heightens the impression of a life
in which public work is sustained by private communion.
  Luke alters Mark's introduction to the story of the healing
of the paralytic. He knocks out Mark's note that this happened at Capernaum and puts in one of his own: that the

opposition is present in the form of *Pharisees and experts in the Law . . . out of every village in Galilee and Judaea as well as from Jerusalem.* This is effective in two ways. It makes the story more tense by pointing to the presence of the opposition at the outset. It gives it a wider setting by saying that these enemies come from all over the country and even from the capital city – this, by the way, being the first hint that the golden Jerusalem of the early chapters is also the city of betrayal and death. *The Lord's power to heal people was with him* – a further note by Luke showing his particular view of Jesus as the man anointed and energized by God and the Spirit.

In telling the story of the paralytic, Luke follows Mark closely. He has done what he wanted to do in the way of heightening the drama and the theology with his little introduction. The connection of physical and moral disease (sin) was an accepted fact then. To cure either of them was a divine action, neither being *easier* than the other. As far as men were concerned, they could only be done by those whom God had appointed. *The Son of Man* is the divinely authorized figure of Daniel 7.13 and 14. A shadowy dream-figure there and in some later writings not in the Old Testament, for the New Testament writers it has become clear: he is Jesus. Again, any reader of Daniel 7 will see its aptness to Christ's resurrection. It is doubtful whether Jesus took such a grandiose title to himself in his lifetime, but the church knew him as the Son of Man, the man who speaks with God's authoritative and creative voice. To leave us in no doubt that God is present in Jesus' saying and doing, Luke adds a note of the spectators' *awe and amazement* to Mark's account – the reaction to God's presence in the world.

5.27–39

27 Later on, Jesus went out and looked straight at a tax-collector called Levi, as he sat in his office.

'Follow me,' he said to him.

28 And he got to his feet, left everything behind and followed him.

29 Then Levi gave a big reception for Jesus in his own house, and there was a great crowd of tax-collectors and others at table with them.

30 The Pharisees and their companions the scribes kept muttering indignantly about this to Jesus' disciples, saying,

'Why do you have your meals with tax-collectors and sinners?'

31 Jesus answered them,

'It is not the healthy who need the doctor, but those who are ill.

32 I did not come with an invitation for the "righteous" but for the "sinners" – to change their ways.'

33 Then people said to him,

'Why is it that John's disciples are always fasting and praying, just like the Pharisees' disciples, but yours both eat and drink?'

34 Jesus answered,

'Can you expect wedding-guests to fast while they have the bridegroom with them?

35 The day will come when they will lose the bridegroom; that will be the time for them to fast!'

36 Then he gave them this illustration.

'Nobody tears a piece from a new coat to patch up an old one. If he does, he ruins the new one and the new piece does not match the old.

37 'Nobody puts new wine into old wineskins. If he does, the new wine will burst the skins – the wine will be spilt and the skins ruined.

38 No, new wine must be put into new wineskins.

39 Of course, nobody who has been drinking old wine will want the new at once. He is sure to say, "The old is a good sound wine".'

By a few deft and economical editorial touches Luke has made this string of incidents much more coherent than it is in Mark, and much easier to read. He strengthens the link between Levi's call and the dinner by making it clear that it is Levi's house and Levi's party. He then joins on the discussion about fasting, making it part of the table-talk, whereas in Mark it is a different scene set nowhere in particular. We see what Luke meant when he talked about getting things into a proper order. He regards Mark as precious, but very raw, material.

Levi's call brings back a gospel theme which is never far away – God's mercy to the disreputable and tainted members of society. He is cut off from decent society by his occupation just as the leper was by his disease. Tax-collectors were not only tools of the Gentile Roman occupation, they were also well known to be in it for what they could get. The modern reader needs to substitute something like 'racketeers and lechers' for Luke's 'tax-collectors and sinners' to get the full flavour of the story. The climax (as is usual in these short incidents) is a saying of Jesus which brings out the theology of the action: God is only concerned with people who need help – the others don't (apparently) need him.

The next section, about fasting, is a collection of proverbs on the theme of new and old which point up the newness of the gospel. The question is: 'Why are Jesus' followers so worldly, so careless about the usual religious practices?' The answer: 'These are not ordinary times. They are like a wedding day when everything else is thrown aside to celebrate a long-awaited resolution' – that refers to the lifetime of Jesus. But soon the disciples are going to have matter for sorrow as well as for joy, and in the church of Luke's day fasting was an accepted custom – hence the addition of the second saying in Mark's gospel.

Two small parables follow on the cue of the tension between the new and the old which has emerged. Luke's version differs from Mark's and Matthew's. The message is the same but Luke's addition of *he ruins the new one* shows a concern for the integrity of Christianity very like St Paul's. He is not going to have it spoiled by the old religion, much though he respects that. To the saying about wine and wine-skins Luke adds his vivid and not unsympathetic sketch of the cosy conservative: *The old is a good sound wine*. He knows what the gospel is up against and the time it will take to establish itself. He is also an admirer of Jewish tradition.

6. 1–11

1   One Sabbath day, as Jesus happened to be passing through the cornfields, his disciples began picking the ears of corn, rubbing them in their hands, and eating them.

2   Some of the Pharisees remarked,

  'Why are you doing what the Law forbids men to do on the Sabbath day?'

3   Jesus answered them and said,

  'Have you never read what David and his men did when they were hungry?

4   He went into the house of God, took the presentation loaves, ate some bread himself and gave some to those with him, even though the Law does not permit anyone except the priests to eat it.'

5   Then he added, 'The Son of Man is master even of the Sabbath.'

6   On another Sabbath day when he went into a syna-gogue to teach, there was a man there whose right hand was wasted away.

7   The scribes and the Pharisees were watching Jesus closely to see whether he would heal on the Sabbath day, which would give them grounds for an accusation.

8   But he knew what was going on in their minds, and said to the man with the wasted hand,

'Stand up and come forward.'

And he got up and stood there.

9   Then Jesus said to them,

'I am going to ask you a question. Does the Law command us to do good on the Sabbath or do harm – to save life or destroy it?'

10   He looked round, meeting all their eyes, and said to the man,

'Now stretch out your hand.'

He did so, and his hand was restored as sound as the other one.

11   But they were filled with insane fury and kept discussing with each other what they could do to Jesus.

These two stories about Jesus and the Sabbath have been lifted from Mark's gospel and set down here by Luke with some small alterations and clarifications. One of them is trivial, the other far-reaching, but in both Jesus confronts the massive wall of legalism and blows holes through it. Legalism, the obsessive desire to do the right thing, springs from a fundamental lack of confidence. When God is felt to be aloof or absent people are particularly anxious to keep the religious rules – there is nothing else for the serious-minded to do. Life becomes like a relationship without trust or grace, or like work without inspiration – stylized, touchy and sad. It is particularly ironical when legalism gets to work on the Sabbath, for this was ordained as a holiday, for the relaxation and refreshment which come from being in the presence of God. No longer certain that God is near, the Pharisees have so buried themselves in the rules about it that they have thwarted its very purpose and spoiled the thing they were trying to protect. Nothing but the presence of God could put this right – and that means Jesus.

The most trivial incidents can spark off the most blazing rows: so in the story of the cornfield. Work was forbidden on

the Sabbath, so the farm-labourers were given a day off
reaping and threshing and their wives a holiday from cook-
ing. But in the eyes of the Pharisees Jesus' disciples are doing
all these things by *picking the ears of corn, rubbing them in their hands,
and eating them*. They could not see anything, not even a
trifling incident like this, outside their preoccupation with
right and wrong. Jesus has two answers. The first turns their
own guns against them: he appeals to an example in the
tradition which they seem to have forgotten – the story about
David in 1 Samuel 24. The past is not the preserve of the
conservatives. The second answer is more explosive: *The Son
of Man is master even of the Sabbath*. The Son of Man is God's
regent and agent, the one to whom he has given his authority
over the earth (see Daniel 7). Probably this verse echoes the
confessing voice of the earliest church's worship.

The second incident, the *man whose right hand was wasted away*,
involves a sharper confrontation with the humanity of God
and leads to an outlook which can only be called 'anti-life'.
This is the issue which Jesus brings into the open, dragging
it out from its respectable coverings: *do good . . . or do harm –
save life or destroy it*? The issue is exposed in a merciless, even
provocative, way. The *insane fury* of the Pharisees comes
from the double humiliation of being beaten and being un-
masked, and the last words make it clear that this story is
not likely to have a clean or happy ending. It is a dramatic
and alarming instance of the two ways in which Luke knows
that God's presence affects people. There is comfort and
healing on one side, and on the other, pain and destruction.

6. 12–19

12   It was in those days that he went up the hillside to
      pray, and spent the whole night in prayer to God.
13   When daylight came, he summoned his disciples to him
      and out of them he chose twelve whom he called
      apostles. They were –

14   Simon (whom he called Peter),
      Andrew, his brother,
      James,
      John,
      Philip.
      Bartholomew,
15   Matthew,
      Thomas,
      James, the son of Alphaeus,
      Simon, called the nationalist,
16   Judas, the son of James, and
      Judas Iscariot, who later betrayed him.
17   Then he came down with them and stood on a level
      piece of ground, surrounded by a large crowd of his
      disciples and a great number of people from all parts of
      Judaea and Jerusalem and the coastal district of Tyre and
      Sidon, who had come to hear him and to be healed of
      their diseases.
18   (And even those who were troubled with evil spirits
      were cured.)
19   The whole crowd were trying to touch him with their
      hands, for power was going out from him and he healed
      them all.

Luke is using material from Mark here, and is building up
to a great discourse very like Matthew's sermon on the
mount. But in spite of his connections with these other
writers he does things his own way. The crowd scene after
the list of the apostles, for example, would come at the
beginning of this passage if Luke were following Mark
exactly, but Luke begins with the twelve. Also the 'geography' here is the opposite of Matthew's. Matthew has
Jesus going *up* the mountain and speaking from there. Luke
has him praying on the mountain and coming *down* to speak.
As our writer is taking so much trouble to arrange his

material in his own particular way, it will be worth following him with equal care.

The overall structure is in the form of a crescendo. From the silent solitude of the first verse, through the gathering of an inner group of apostles, to the clamorous public scene of the last verses there is a gradual build-up. Geography, or sense of place, plays an important part; and here it is important to bear in mind that for the gospel-writers this was not just matter of fact but symbolic. He went up the mountain to pray. Why say *the* mountain? Which mountain, then? The answer is: the mountain of God. Mountains were the places where God spoke to men and drew near to them. The mountain here is Sinai on which God gave Moses the Law, or Horeb where he met Elijah. This is *the* mountain. Luke uses it as the scene for the communion of God and man *praying* in the wonder and peace of the *night*. Then, as the sun comes up, twelve more characters come on to the stage. These are the 'eye-witnesses and teachers of the message' whom Luke spoke of in the introduction. They are *summoned* by Jesus and do not come of their own choice. They are *called apostles*, which means 'sent men': both officers of the church and typical Christians. Notice the position of this incident in the scheme: on the one side the apostles are linked to Jesus' communion with God in prayer, on the other to his work in the world of healing and teaching. They belong to both. They are with him on the mountain and on the plain – Christian living in a nutshell.

Then he came down with them to the plain. Literally and symbolically Luke brings the story down to earth, to the place where people live and do their ordinary business. His reference to the wide areas from which the crowd comes underlines this. We have noticed that the movement is directly opposite to Matthew's at this point (see Matthew 5.1). This puts Jesus and his teaching on a (literally) less elevated plane than Matthew where Jesus, like God, speaks on the mountain. Here he is more like Moses bringing God's words down from Sinai to the people below. But we remember that we started on the mountain and that the scene on the plain has its own power and wonder: *power was going out from him*, Luke says. The advantage of Luke's way of doing things is that the word is spoken in our familiar world. That is why he has kept Mark's crowd scene aside until now. The 'beyond' and the secret word which is with God in the quiet communion of prayer, comes down to be among us.

'Great things are done when men and mountains meet;
This is not done by jostling in the street.'

William Blake

– that is Matthew's point of view. Luke wants to connect the mysteries of the kingdom with the jostling in the street.

6.20–38

20 Then Jesus looked steadily at his disciples and said,
    'How happy are you who own nothing, for the kingdom of God is yours!

21 'How happy are you who are hungry now, for you will be satisfied!
    'How happy are you who weep now, for you are going to laugh!

22 'How happy are you when men hate you and turn you out of their company; when they slander you and reject all that you stand for because you are loyal to the Son of Man.

23 Be glad when that happens and jump for joy – your reward in Heaven is magnificent. For that is exactly how their fathers treated the prophets.

24 'But how miserable for you who are rich, for you have had all your comforts!

25 'How miserable for you who have all you want, for you are going to be hungry!

'How miserable for you who are laughing now, for you will know sorrow and tears!

26 'How miserable for you when everybody praises you, for that is exactly how their fathers treated the false prophets.

27 'But I say to all of you who will listen to me: love your enemies, do good to those who hate you,

28 bless those who curse you, and pray for those who treat you spitefully.

29 'As for the man who hits you on one cheek, offer him the other one as well! And if a man is taking away your coat, do not stop him from taking your shirt as well.

30 Give to everyone who asks you, and when a man has taken what belongs to you, don't demand it back.

31 'Treat men exactly as you would like them to treat you.

32 If you love only those who love you, what credit is that to you? Even sinners love those who love them!

33 And if you do good only to those who do good to you, what credit is that to you? Even sinners do that much.

34 And if you lend only to those from whom you hope to get your money back, what credit is that to you? Even sinners lend to sinners and expect to get their money back.

35 No, you are to love your *enemies* and do good and lend without hope of return. Your reward will be wonderful and you will be sons of the Most High. For he is kind to the ungrateful and the wicked!

36 'You must be merciful, as your Father is merciful.

37 Don't judge other people and you will not be judged yourselves. Don't condemn and you will not be condemned. Forgive others and people will forgive you.

38 Give and men will give to you – yes, good measure, pressed down, shaken together and running over will they pour into your lap. For whatever measure you use

with other people, they will use in their dealings with you.'

Here Luke stops following Mark and prefers Matthew, so the best way to find out what he is doing is to compare his work with Matthew's – in this instance with the Sermon on the Mount of Matthew 5–7. We have already noticed the significance of the different places where this preaching is done, the plain as against the mountain. We can see at a glance that Luke's discourse is much the shorter of the two, though it begins and ends in the same way. Probably he does not want to interrupt the action and the story for too long. Some of Matthew's material he leaves out, some he puts by to use later. The parts that he neglects are to do with the more technical sides of church life like alms-giving and fasting. Those that he puts by will be worked into the action here and there and not put in one block. This leaves him with sayings of Jesus which illustrate the human conse-quences of the life he brings. He puts them more in ordinary life and less in the Christian fold than Matthew.

Then Jesus looked steadily at his disciples and said . . . It is essential to notice who this is for. These are not general worldly truths. Indeed, from the worldly point of view they are not true at all. They are for those who accept the new life of the kingdom of God which is not the kingdoms of the world (remember the temptation story). They are for those who intend to live from that and for it. Only in that living will the sayings be found to be true.

How happy are you . . . *How miserable for you* . . . Luke has only four 'beatitudes' against Matthew's eight, but he matches them with something Matthew does not have, the four woes. From the Magnificat onwards he has used a double-edged theology. The gospel means joy to some and misery to others. The good news is for the poor – that was made clear at the outset of Jesus' work – not just because they are poor

but because their poverty cries out for something to fill it.
The bad news is for the rich, not just because they are rich
but because their lives are satisfactory and they do not want
anything else. But, unlike Matthew, when Luke mentions
poverty and hunger he does not mean 'spiritual' conditions.
He is talking about the real thing. These blessings and these
woes are hard facts – not, however, grounded in worldly
values but in the God who reverses the worldly order. They
cannot be read out of the state of things as they are at present.
They belong to a promised future: so they can only be really
understood in faith and in hope.

The blessings and woes are followed by a series of little
pictures which show God's reversal of worldly practice being
acted out by ordinary people to show what life is like when
God is in it. The keynote is a divinely reckless generosity
worked out in human terms, so uncalculating that it gives a
touch of surprise and grace to the most humdrum trans-
actions. *You are to love your enemies* – that is the essence of
Christian living, but if it were something which one decided
to do as a moral exercise it would certainly come out in a
patronizing, insincere and heavy-handed manner. But it is
not like that. It springs not from a man's efforts but from his
glad apprehension of God's exuberant kindness and mercy.
We behave like this because he is like this – which means, in
the end, that life is like this: *You must be merciful, as your Father is
merciful.* To get the flavour of what such a life would be like,
notice the juicily sensuous image of abundance in the words
(only in Luke) *good measure, pressed down, shaken together and running
over will they pour into your lap.* It is a more demanding, yet much
happier life than the ordinary – more careful and more
careless.

6.39–49

39　　Then he gave them an illustration –
　　　'Can one blind man be guide to another blind man?

Surely they will both fall into the ditch.

40 A disciple is not above his teacher, but when he is fully trained he will be like his teacher.

41 'Why do you look at the speck of sawdust in your brother's eye and fail to notice the plank in your own?

42 How can you say to your brother, "Let me take the speck out of your eye" when you cannot see the plank in your own? You fraud, take the plank out of your own eye first and then you can see clearly to remove the speck out of your brother's eye.

43 'It is impossible for a good tree to produce bad fruit – as impossible as it is for a bad tree to produce good fruit.

44 Do not men know what a tree is by its fruit? You cannot pick figs from briars, or gather a bunch of grapes from a blackberry bush!

45 A good man produces good things from the good stored up in his heart, and a bad man produces evil things from his own stores of evil. For a man's words express what overflows from his heart.

46 'And what is the point of calling me, "Lord, Lord", without doing what I tell you to do?

47 Let me show you what the man who comes to me, hears what I have to say, and puts it into practice, is really like.

48 He is like a man building a house, who dug down to rock-bottom and laid the foundation of his house upon it. Then when the flood came and the flood-water swept down upon that house, it could not shift it because it was properly built.

49 But the man who hears me and does not act upon what he hears is like a man who built his house upon soft earth without foundation. When the flood-water swept down upon it, it collapsed and the whole house crashed down in ruins.'

The proclamation of generosity is followed by a biting and satirical critique of what often passes for serious and religious living. This passage relies on words of Jesus found in Matthew, a collection of apothegms which expose the falsehood of a high-minded life which owes nothing to the light, mercy and goodness of the gospel.

The first saying about the blind man and the status of a disciple are not in the Sermon on the Mount in Matthew but in sections dealing with the Pharisees and the mission of the twelve. Luke includes them here because they fit in with his theme of blindness and guidance, a warning against those who want to rush into the religious life without having learned anything about themselves. The second saying emphasizes it with a picture of a man who can scarcely see himself attempting the exacting business of trying to remove a tiny speck from someone else's eye – a foolish and very dangerous enterprise.

The illustration, or little parable, of trees and their fruit says the same thing in a different image. The heart is the source of our doing and thinking. Attempts to be better or other than we are there at the centre are useless and muddling. Both the good and the bad life have a sort of inevitability about them. Murder will out, and goodness will out. This is the fulfilment of old Simeon's alarming prophecy that Jesus *will expose the secret thoughts of many hearts*.

In case the reader was supposing that Christian life is just an internal attitude, the last paragraph puts him right. Calling 'Lord, Lord' may be correct theology and enthusiastic worship, but it counts for nothing without obedience expressed in deeds. Religion has to be soundly earthed in practical action if it is going to stand up under examination and pressure.

7. 1–10

1   When Jesus had finished these talks to the people, he came to Capernaum,

2   where it happened that there was a man very seriously ill and in fact at the point of death. He was the slave of a centurion who thought very highly of him.

3   When the centurion heard about Jesus, he sent some Jewish elders to him with the request that he would come and save his slave's life.

4   When they came to Jesus, they urged him strongly to grant this request, saying that the centurion deserved to have this done for him.

5   'He loves our nation and has built us a synagogue out of his own pocket,' they said.

6   So Jesus went with them, but as he approached the house, the centurion sent some of his friends with the message,

'Don't trouble yourself, sir! I'm not important enough for you to come into my house –

7   I didn't think I was fit to come to you in person. Just give the order, please, and my boy will recover.

8   I am used to working under orders, and I have soldiers under me. I can say to one, "Go", and he goes, or I can say to another, "Come here", and he comes; or I can say to my slave, "Do this job", and he does it.'

9   These words amazed Jesus and he turned to the crowd who were following him and said,

'I have never found faith like this anywhere, even in Israel!'

10   Then those who had been sent by the centurion returned to the house and found the slave perfectly well.

This story is on the same pattern as Matthew (8. 5–13) and John (4. 46–53). The early Christians no doubt treasured it as a dramatic picture of a direct and perfect faith in action. This is nothing more nor less than a conviction that God can do things, that his word is not just talk but takes effect. The story of the resurrection at Nain which comes next will demonstrate this doctrine of the creative word of God. The centurion lives in a world where words are not toys but result in things happening. When he gets an order he acts on it, when he gives one it is carried out without question. Words and deeds go together with him. This is genuine faith – believing and doing.

While Luke has nothing to add to the central message of this traditional story, his filling-in of the background shows his particular interests as a Jewish Christian looking out to the wider Gentile world. As well as being an example of faith, the centurion is, for him, a figure of the kind of sympathetic outsiders whom he has in mind in writing his book – a bridge-character connecting the Jewish and Gentile worlds. This is why Luke inserts the details about his benevolence and sympathy towards the Jews. He is so like Cornelius in Acts that he is almost the same person. But it is important to remember that Luke's purpose in writing is not to bring Jews and Gentiles together in a generally charitable way. First and foremost he is proclaiming Jesus Christ. He is the one in whom different kinds of men come together, the place of their belonging to one another. (See Ephesians 2.11–16 for a more generalized expression of this teaching.) The delegation of Jewish elders which brings the centurion's request shows that Jewish and Gentile interests coincide in the need for the salvation (= 'health' in Greek) and new life which Jesus can give. In him 'there is neither Jew nor Greek, for you are all one' (Galatians 3.28). The delegation does something else too. It keeps the centurion off-stage. Luke is quite clear that he is writing about Jesus' ministry to the Jews. The time of the Gentiles comes later and he will deal with it fully in Acts, so it suits his overall scheme that Jesus and the centurion should not meet as they do in Matthew's version and in John's (the nobleman). It is not yet the right time for it, and Luke believes that God's revelation of himself is in the sequence of history. Things have their times and their places.

7. 11–17

11   Not long afterwards, Jesus went into a town called Nain, accompanied by his disciples and a large crowd.

12   As he approached the city gate, it happened that some people were carrying out a dead man, the only son of his widowed mother. The usual crowd of fellow-townsmen was with her.

13   When the Lord saw her, his heart went out to her and he said,

> 'Don't cry.'

14   Then he walked up and put his hand on the bier while the bearers stood still. Then he said,

> 'Young man, get up!'

15   And the dead man sat up and began to talk, and Jesus handed him to his mother.

16   Everybody present was awe-struck and they praised God, saying,

> 'A great prophet has arisen among us and God has turned his face towards his people.'

17   And this report of him spread through the whole of Judaea and the surrounding countryside.

Luke is the only gospel-writer who tells us this story. If he is giving pure historical facts it is very strange that such a startling and conclusive demonstration of Jesus' power and divinity should either have been ignored by the other evangelists or forgotten in the traditions they used. The stories of the raising of Lazarus in John and of the ruler's daughter in the first three gospels tell us that a tradition of

Jesus raising the dead was widespread in the early church, but it also tells us that this had no one hard and fast historical form. Since speculation about what actually happened is not going to get us far, how should this passage be read?

First we should remember, as we have done before, that Luke is writing after the resurrection of Jesus, in the light of the resurrection of Jesus and because of the resurrection of Jesus. This applies to him as much as it does to St Paul, the difference between them being only that Paul presents his theology in the form of argument and Luke presents his in the form of story. But for both of them the resurrection is the centre of life. It will therefore be reasonable and illuminating to read this passage not as historical reportage but as a description of what it is to become a Christian, namely to be raised up by Christ from a life so hopeless that it amounts to death, and to be given back to ordinary life and relationships by his hand (*and Jesus handed him to his mother*).

Anyone who reads 1 Kings 17 (the story of Elijah raising a widow's only son and giving him back to her) will see that this has had so great an influence on Luke at this point that it is virtually his major source. In fact, Luke makes this quite plain by having the crowd exclaim: *A great prophet has arisen among us*. That 'prophet' can only be Elijah and it means that Jesus is like him, the great prophet who will come before the last day (see Malachi 4.5: 'I will send you Elijah the prophet before the great and terrible day of the Lord comes'). In the baptism scene Luke took care not to follow Mark in making John the Baptist like Elijah by leaving out the description of his appearance (Mark 1.6 which refers back to 2 Kings 1.8). This is part of Luke's view of history: more spaced-out and less compressed than Mark's. In Mark John is the new Elijah who comes just before the end. Jesus is the end. Luke seems to have pushed everything back one place, leaving a space free for his third period of history – the church. So John is part of the old order (16.16), Jesus is the herald and establisher of the new order but is not the end, for there is a further phase of history still to come in the Acts of the Apostles. Luke can compare Jesus to Elijah because he does not bring life in the world to a close but rather initiates a new and continuous form of life in the world, an existence which starts with resurrection and journeys towards the last day.

God has turned his face towards his people echoes Zachariah's song precisely. Now it is happening.

7. 18–35

18 John's disciples reported all these happenings to him.
19 Then he summoned two of them and sent them to the Lord with this message,

'Are you the one who is to come, or are we to look for someone else?'

20 When the men came to Jesus, they said,

'John the Baptist has sent us to you with this message, "Are you the one who is to come, or are we to look for someone else?" '

21 At that very time Jesus was healing many people of their diseases and ailments and evil spirits, and he restored sight to many who were blind.

22 Then he answered them,

'Go and tell John what you have seen and heard. The blind are recovering their sight, cripples are walking again, lepers being healed, the deaf hearing, dead men are being brought to life again, and the good news is being given to those in need.

23 And happy is the man who never loses his faith in me.'

24 When these messengers had gone back, Jesus began to talk to the crowd about John.

'What did you go out into the desert to look at? Was it a reed waving in the breeze?

25 Well, *what* was it you went out to see? A man dressed in

fine clothes? But the men who wear fine clothes live luxuriously in palaces.

26 But what *did* you really go to see? A prophet? Yes, I tell you, a prophet and far more than a prophet!

27 This is the man of whom the scripture says,

> Behold, I send my messenger before thy face,
> Who shall prepare thy way before thee.

28 'Believe me, no one greater than John has ever been born, and yet a humble member of the kingdom of God is greater than he.

29 'All the people, yes, even the tax-collectors, when they heard John, acknowledged God and were baptized by his baptism.

30 But the Pharisees and the experts in the Law frustrated God's purpose for them, for they refused John's baptism.

31 'What can I say that the men of this generation are like – what sort of men are they?

32 They are like children sitting in the market-place and calling out to each other, "We played at weddings for you, but you wouldn't dance, and we played at funerals for you, and you wouldn't cry!"

33 For John the Baptist came in the strictest austerity and you say he is crazy.

34 Then the Son of Man came, enjoying food and drink, and you say, "Look, a drunkard and a glutton, a bosom-friend of the tax-collector and the outsider!"

35 So wisdom is proved right by all her children!'

The aim of Luke's book is to face his readers with Jesus Christ and so bring them to decide about him and his religion. His usual way of doing this is by narratives like the two which come before this passage; but he uses discussion and argument too, just as he used the songs in the first two chapters, as a way of bringing out the underlying issues. In the same way a dramatist will make a lull in the action so that the characters can reflect on the significance of what has happened, come to decisions about it, and enable the audience to do the same. John the Baptist is not brought into the story for his own sake but to answer the question 'Who is Jesus?' John is clearly a very impressive man. But for all that Jesus says: *Believe me, no one greater than John has ever been born, and yet a humble member of the kingdom of God is greater than he.* Chapters 1 and 2 made that clear: the kingdom of God begins with Jesus. Luke sees it in Christian terms.

Are you the one . . . or are we to look for someone else? The question is answered by actions and words which mean that Jesus is all that a man needs to know, that a man is happy if he sticks to Jesus and never gives up following him, for he is the one who does the healing work of God.

Jesus goes on to acknowledge the greatness of John. Those who attended to him and obeyed him by being baptized did the right thing. Characteristically, it was not the respectable religious authorities but the riff-raff who thus *acknowledged God.*

Luke's gospel is more worldly than the others while keeping the demand for asceticism. There are those, however, who never come to a decision about either. They find it more dignified (and much safer) to criticize what is going on from outside. It is this sort of attitude which Jesus satirizes and ridicules in his words about the men of this generation – some people are never satisfied. The sterility of such diplomatic immunity is exposed. It means not being prepared to do anything whole-heartedly, to let oneself go in weeping or laughing, in all-out effort or in abandoned play. Yet wisdom (i.e. God's wisdom – revealed by Christ) is vindicated by all her children, her hermits and her comedians. Only the stand-offish are strangers to it, the real fools.

36   Then one of the Pharisees asked Jesus to a meal with him. When Jesus came into the house, he took his place at the table

37 and a woman, known in the town as a bad character, found out that Jesus was there and brought an alabaster flask of perfume

38 and stood behind him crying, letting her tears fall on his feet and then drying them with her hair.

39 Then she kissed them and anointed them with the perfume. When the Pharisee who had invited him saw this, he said to himself, 'If this man were really a prophet, he would know who this woman is and what sort of a person is touching him. He would have realized that she is a bad woman.'

40 Then Jesus spoke to him,

    'Simon, there is something I want to say to you.'

    'Very well, Master,' he returned, 'say it.'

41   'Once upon a time, there were two men in debt to the same money-lender. One owed him fifty pounds and the other five.

42 And since they were unable to pay, he generously cancelled both of their debts. Now, which one of them do you suppose will love him more?'

43   'Well,' returned Simon, 'I suppose it will be the one who has been more generously treated.'

    'Exactly,' replied Jesus,

44 and then turning to the woman, he said to Simon,

    'You see this woman? I came into your house but you provided no water to wash my feet. But she has washed my feet with her tears and dried them with her hair.

45 You gave me no kiss of welcome, but she, from the moment I came in, has not stopped covering my feet with kisses.

46   You gave me no oil for my head, but she has put perfume on my feet.

47   That is why I tell you, Simon, that her sins, many as they are, are forgiven; for she has so much love. But the man who has little to be forgiven has only a little love to give.'

48   Then he said to her,
        'Your sins are forgiven.'

49   And the men at table with him began to say to themselves,
        'And who is this man, who even forgives sins?'

50   But Jesus said to the woman,
        'It is your faith that has saved you. Go in peace.'

1   Not long after this incident, Jesus went through every town and village preaching and telling the people the good news of the kingdom of God. He was accompanied by the twelve

2   and some women who had been cured of evil spirits and illnesses – Mary, known as 'the woman from Magdala' (who had once been possessed by seven evil spirits),

3   Joanna the wife of Chuza, an agent of Herod, Susanna, and many others who used to look after Jesus' and his companions' comfort from their own resources.

Look, a drunkard and a glutton, a bosom-friend of the tax-collector and the outsider! The resentful charge against himself, which Jesus took up and flung back, is still reverberating. So is his indictment of his respectable detractors who prefer to stand aside and criticize rather than join in anything difficult or delightful. This story shows it all happening by dramatizing the triangle of relationships Jesus–Pharisees–sinners in a way which makes it so immediate and inescapable that readers are forced to identify and take sides.

Luke has been quite deliberate. He takes a story from Mark,

lifts it from the end of Jesus' ministry to the middle, and changes and amplifies it so brilliantly that his version is the one people remember. Mark only tells us of an incident at dinner in Bethany in the house of Simon the Leper, of how a woman came and poured precious ointment from an alabaster box on to Jesus' head, how the others were annoyed at the waste and how Jesus accepted it as a good work, pointing forward to his burial. In Luke everything except the skeleton of the tale is different. The house is *Simon the Pharisee's*, the woman is a *sinner*, and it is this which annoys the other people present. Jesus accepts what she has done as an act of *love* and penitence, and this (rather than its pointing towards his death) is the story's value and significance. But perhaps Luke's greatest contribution and the reason why his is the memorable version is the greater emotional perception which he brings to Mark's stark little narrative. He tells us of the weeping and the kissing, the resentment in Simon's heart, the psychological connection of loving generosity with forgiveness.

If this man were really a prophet . . . He would have realized that she is a bad woman. The description of Jesus as a prophet reminds us of the incident at Nain where Jesus' divine power was shown. So here is a great religious figure – that has been recognized. Then why does he not behave as a great religious figure should, knowing the difference between good and bad? The answer is that Jesus goes deeper than morals, deeper even than religion, to the human heart. In the woman he sees that generously self-forgetting love which can come from those whose pride has been so humbled by their failings that they are no longer concerned with their own status or respectability. Forgiveness is the only remaining possibility for such, and love (not pride or detraction) the only feasible relationship. In Simon he sees the opposite: the cold and envious resentment which is at the centre of so many well-preserved lives which are too comfortably self-concerned to go out to others except in criticism – *You gave me no kiss of welcome.* Once again we remember the Magnificat: *he has swept away the high and mighty . . . and lifted up the humble.* And Simeon's prophecy: *this child is destined to make many fall and many rise in Israel.* For the Simon in every man the gospel is a nasty shock, but for the humiliated sinner in him it is salvation, peace and a new start.

To this searching and unforgettable story Luke adds the general note of 8. 1–3 which restores the overall narrative line and brings us back into public life. There is theological point to Jesus' being accompanied by the twelve who incorporate the future church. The women are held up as examples of how ladies of means can make themselves useful to the cause.

8.4–15

4   When a large crowd had collected and people were coming to him from one town after another, he spoke to them and gave them this parable:

5   'A sower went out to sow his seed, and while he was sowing, some of the seed fell by the roadside and was trodden down and the birds gobbled it up.

6   Some fell on the rock, and when it sprouted it withered for lack of moisture.

7   Some fell among thorn-bushes which grew up with the seeds and choked the life out of them.

8   And some seed fell on good soil and grew and produced a crop – a hundred times what had been sown.'

    And when he had said this, he called out,

    'Let the man who has ears to hear use them!'

9   Then his disciples asked him the meaning of the parable.

10   To which Jesus replied,

    'You have been given the privilege of understanding

the secrets of the kingdom of God, but the others are given parables so that they may go through life with their eyes open and see nothing, and with their ears open, and understand nothing of what they hear.

11 'This is what the parable means. The seed is the message of God.

12 The seed sown by the roadside represents those who hear the message, and then the devil comes and takes it away from their hearts so that they cannot believe it and be saved.

13 That sown on the rock represents those who accept the message with great delight when they hear it, but have no real root. They believe for a little while but when the time of temptation comes, they lose faith.

14 And the seed sown among the thorns represents the people who hear the message and go on their way, and with the worries and riches and pleasures of living, the life is choked out of them, and in the end they produce nothing.

15 But the seed sown on good soil means the men who hear the message and grasp it with a good and honest heart, and go on steadily producing a good crop.

Now Luke is back with Mark as his source, but he does not pick him up precisely where he had left him. He puts the Beelzebub dispute aside for the present and begins again with the parable of the sower instead. He does this, deliberately as always, because its message of the mixed reception given to the gospel connects with the preceding story of Jesus, the Pharisee and the bad woman, amplifying and developing a theme which began at 7.31. Underlying this parable about seed is a problem shared by Jesus, the early church and any convinced believer: the truth has come – why do so few people receive it?

The Marcan original is an allegory which centres on the

mystery of God (Mark 4.11). Around this leading theme of Mark's cluster other concerns of his: refusal of the gospel, persecution, fulfilment through loss. It is a promise to a church under fire that the transforming power of God will bring about an inconceivably glorious resolution.

But all that is very much Mark, and Luke has other concerns. It is not the central mystery which interests him: he follows Matthew in changing it into *mysteries* which is weaker, and he diminishes Mark's resounding climax to both parable and interpretation by abbreviating or jettisoning the triumphant incantation: 'Thirty-fold, sixty-fold, hundred-fold.' This leaves the focus of interest on the different reactions to *the word of God*, which is just what we would expect of the narrator who is more interested in the intelligible progress of God's will in human history than in the dark paradox at the heart of theology. Luke has, in fact, read Mark as many modern readers and preachers do, missing the mystery and fixing on the allegorical moralizing of the different soils or characters. This has its uses and is an obvious enough course of action, but this is a moment when we may regret that the sense and plausibility of the Lucan approach has gilded over odder and deeper apprehensions.

8.16–21

16 'Nobody lights a lamp and covers it with a basin or puts it under the bed. No, a man puts his lamp on a lamp-stand so that those who come in can see the light.
17 For there is nothing hidden now which will not become perfectly plain and there are no secrets now which will not become as clear as daylight.
18 So take care how you listen – more will be given to the man who has something already, but the man who has nothing will lose even what he thinks he has.'
19 Then his mother and his brothers arrived to see him,

but could not get near him because of the crowd.
20   So a message was passed to him,
        'Your mother and your brothers are standing outside
     wanting to see you.'
21   To which he replied,
        'My mother and my brothers? They are those who
     listen to God's message and obey it.'

Mark was the writer who collected these miscellaneous but
unforgettable sayings of Jesus together, and Luke takes over
his arrangement. It is hard to see any clear connection
between them or with what comes before and what follows.
Possibly they should be seen as a development of what it
means to be one of those who accept the word *with a good
and honest heart*. The reader of Luke's gospel will certainly be
reminded of Simeon's prophecy of the uncovering of the
secrets of men's hearts when he reads verse 17. Luke has added
the words *so that those who come in can see the light*. They give us a
picture of the church as a house with open doors, the light
within serving to guide and greet outsiders as they enter.
This contrasts with Matthew's version, *it gives light for everybody
in the house*, which betrays a more inward-looking view of the
church than Luke's.

The incident concerning Jesus' mother and brothers shows
us how far we have come since Chapter 2. Jesus is no longer
tied to the family. The important and governing relationships of his life are now with *those who listen to God's message and
obey it*. For the many Christians of Luke's day who had had
to make a similar break this will have been confirming and
encouraging. Sentimentality about the family in today's
church should not obscure the fact that the gospel brings
independence from natural ties and sets a man in a new and
wider web of love and duty.

8.22–40

22   It happened on one of these days that he got into a boat with his disciples and said to them,

'Let us cross over to the other side of the lake.'

So they set sail,

23 and when they were under way he fell asleep. Then a squall of wind swept down upon the lake and they were in grave danger of being swamped.

24 Coming forward, they woke him up, saying,

'Master, master, we're drowning!'

Then he got up and reprimanded the wind and the stormy waters, and they died down, and everything was still.

25 Then he said to them,

'What has happened to your faith?'

But they were frightened and bewildered and kept saying to each other,

'Who ever can this be? He gives orders even to the winds and waters and they obey him.'

26   They sailed on to the country of Gergesenes which is on the opposite side of the lake to Galilee.

27 And as Jesus disembarked, a man from the town who was possessed by evil spirits met him. He had worn no clothes for a long time and did not live inside a house, but among the tombs.

28 When he saw Jesus, he let out a howl and fell down in front of him, yelling,

'What have you got to do with me, you Jesus, Son of the Most High God? Please, please, don't torment me.'

29   For Jesus was commanding the evil spirit to come out of the man. Again and again the evil spirits had taken control of him, and though he was bound with chains and fetters and closely watched, he would snap his bonds and go off into the desert with the devil at his heels.

30   Then Jesus asked him,
        'What is your name?'
        'Legion!' he replied. For many evil spirits had gone
     into him,

31   and were now begging Jesus not to order them off to the
     bottomless pit.

32   It happened that there was a large herd of pigs feeding
     on the hillside, so they implored him to allow them to
     go into the pigs, and he let them go.

33   And when the evil spirits came out of the man and went
     into the pigs, the whole herd stampeded down the cliff
     into the lake and was drowned.

34   When the swineherds saw what had happened, they took
     to their heels, pouring out the story to the people in
     the town and countryside.

35   These people came out to see what had happened, and
     approached Jesus. They found the man, whom the evil
     spirits had left, sitting down at Jesus' feet, properly
     clothed and quite sane. That frightened them.

36   Those who had seen it told the others how the man
     with the evil spirits had been cured.

37   And the whole crowd of people from the district sur-
     rounding the Gergesenes' country begged Jesus to go
     away from them, for they were thoroughly frightened.
     Then he re-embarked on the boat and turned back.

38   The man who had had the evil spirits kept begging to go
     with Jesus, but he sent him away with the words,

39   'Go back home and tell them all that God has done
     for you.'
        So the man went away and told the story of what
     Jesus had done for him, all over the town.

40   On Jesus' return, the crowd welcomed him back, for
     they had all been looking for him.

'Who dost still the roaring of the seas, the roaring of

their waves, the tumult of the peoples.' That quotation
from Psalm 65 gives a clue to the conjunction of these two
stories. Both deal with menacing disorder in the natural and
human worlds and show Jesus as the one who can overcome
it. The two incidents should therefore be read together.

Nobody in the ancient world went to sea for pleasure. The
Book of Jonah and Psalm 107.23–30 (which probably lies
behind this story) give some idea of how the Jews felt about
it – a hostile, uncontrollable and threatening element which
was no friend of men. For this reason the image of the sea has
a significant place in Jewish theology. There could be no more
telling sign of God's power than his supremacy over the
waters. Psalm 104 is a version of the creation story which
graphically describes God's word putting the sea in its place.
It is anti-man and in some way anti-God, for it represents
chaos. The great difference is that man can do nothing
about it – but God can. All this points up the disciples'
astonished question, *Who ever can this be? He gives orders even to
the winds and waters and they obey him* – and it requires a shattering
(but unspoken) answer. *What has happened to your faith?* i.e. to
faith like the centurion's that God's word is authoritative
and effective in his world, that 'God's word for all their craft
and force one moment will not linger' (Luther). The weight
of this story is thus decidedly theological and symbolic rather
than historical, and it is best read accordingly.

The next incident gives us a vivid picture of disordered
humanity. Man under sin is distracted by alien powers
which run him to destruction. He is a menace to himself
and to everybody else. The *tombs* (death) are his natural
habitat. Civilized Luke has added *did not live inside a house* as an
extra touch of horror. As in the first miracle at Capernaum,
the evil spirits recognize Jesus immediately and are terrified
and abject. They implore him not to put an end to their
parasitic existence by sending them back where they belong –
the bottomless pit. Jesus' letting them go *into the pigs* is not the

concession which it appears, for the pigs carry them *into the lake*. So they end up in the bottomless pit (literally 'the abyss') after all. Luke has added two touches of his own to what remains of the Mark story. The cured man is found *sitting down at Jesus' feet* – an image of sanity which will recur in the Mary and Martha story in Chapter 10. The Gerasene people are *thoroughly frightened* – the stock reaction to God's mighty works in this gospel. They do not want this disturbing character in their neighbourhood. The man is sent back to ordinary life to proclaim God's power and kindness there.

8.41–56

41 Then up came Jairus (who was president of the synagogue), and fell at Jesus' feet, begging him to come into his house,

42 for his daughter, an only child of about twelve years old, was dying.

But as he went, the crowds nearly suffocated him.

43 Among them was a woman, who had had a chronic haemorrhage for twelve years and who had derived no benefit from anybody's treatment.

44 She came up behind Jesus and touched the edge of his cloak, and her haemorrhage stopped at once.

45 'Who was that who touched me?' said Jesus.

And when everybody denied it, Peter remonstrated,

'Master, the crowds are all round you and are pressing you on all sides. . . .'

46 But Jesus said,

'Somebody touched me, for I felt that power went out from me.'

47 When the woman realized that she had not escaped notice she came forward trembling, and fell at his feet and admitted before everybody why she had had to touch him, and how she had been instantly cured.

48 'Daughter,' said Jesus, 'it is your faith that has healed you – go in peace.'

49 While he was still speaking, somebody came from the synagogue president's house to say,
'Your daughter is dead – there is no need to trouble the master any further.'

50 But when Jesus heard this, he said to him,
'Now don't be afraid, go on believing and she will be all right.'

51 Then when he came to the house, he would not allow anyone to go in with him except Peter, John and James, and the child's parents.

52 All those already there were weeping and wailing over her, but he said,
'Stop crying! She is not dead, she is fast asleep.'

53 This drew a scornful laugh from them, for they were quite certain that she had died.

54 But he took the little girl's hand and called out to her,
'Get up, my child!'

55 And her spirit came back and she got to her feet at once, and Jesus told them to give her some food.

56 Her parents were nearly out of their minds with joy, but Jesus told them not to tell anyone what had happened.

Piling one miracle story on another could be tedious. The sandwiching of two together which we have here makes more exciting reading. We owe this touch of dramatic skill to Mark who used this arrangement more than once. Luke is glad to take it up, only embroidering it with a few touches of his own which are worth pointing out.

The welcoming and expectant crowd at the beginning is typical of him and reflects his confident belief in a world waiting for the Christian gospel and receiving it gladly. It is equally characteristic of Luke, with his consciousness of

time, to add a note about someone's age. Twelve was the
turning-point between childhood and maturity (cf. Jesus at
2.42), so to die at that point was particularly tragic. It may
also have been suggested to him by the other twelve in the
story, the length of the woman's illness. The woman's shy-
ness is explained by the fact that her disease made her ritually
unclean. But she has the faith which allows the possibility
of a transformation, believing that Jesus has the power to
change things. *I felt that power went out from me* reminds us of
Mark 5.29. Only Luke puts into Jesus' mouth this very
physical idea of Jesus as the source of healing, as if his body
were charged with something like electricity. (Cf. the *bodily
form* of the spirit at Jesus' baptism.) Perhaps (but less likely)
he has in mind the common experience that answering the
needs of others 'takes it out of you'. Notice how Luke brings
in the crowd again by adding *before everybody*.

Peter, John and James are often chosen to be present at
great moments (5.10, the miraculous catch, 9.28, the transfiguration), probably because they represent the Christian
community as witnesses of the resurrection. Luke's *her spirit
came back* is an Old Testament phrase reflecting the view that
human life depends on the spirit breathed into it by God.

After all these bits and pieces of notes some more unified
comment is called for. Jesus is shown as the source of healing
and new life, there for all who need it and want it. But this
wanting is precisely the point. Really to want and to insist
on getting what one asks for amounts, in Luke's view, to
faith. Whether a person comes demonstratively like Jairus
or diffidently like the woman it is their passionate openness
which allows God to act.

5

The Turning-Point

It is helpful to look at 9.1–10.20 as a unit. In the middle of it is the turning-point in the gospel story in which glory and shame come together in the transfiguration and the purposeful setting out to certain death at Jerusalem. On either side of this momentous watershed there are scenes in which Jesus sends out followers to do his work, twelve in the first instance and seventy in the second. Since Luke is the only gospel-writer to have *two* such scenes, and since they frame the centre or axis of his gospel,[4] we can be sure that he is up to something. What? Time and again we have noticed his interest in historical progression, his way of linking one thing to another. Here he is tying the history of the church, represented by the twelve and the seventy, into the history of Jesus. It is not only Jesus' story that he is telling but the church's too, and in this way the Christian community is linked to the splendour and the suffering of the gospel. The teaching of Jesus in Chapter 9 insists on this very thing (especially 9.23–27). The tie-up of Christians with Christ is made particularly strong by being done on *both* sides of the main transfiguration block. The increase in the number of followers from twelve in the first instance to seventy in the second is an expression of Luke's theme of the widening scope of the gospel – but note that it widens only through the paradox of losing life to find it.

4. As did the two feedings for Mark – Luke has reduced them to one.

9. I–10

1   Then he called the twelve together and gave them
     power and authority over all evil spirits and the ability
     to heal disease.

2   He sent them out to preach the kingdom of God and to
     heal the sick, with these words,

3   'Take nothing for your journey – neither a stick nor a
     purse nor food nor money, nor even extra clothes!

4   When you come to stay at a house, remain there until
     you go on your way again.

5   And where they will not welcome you, leave that town,
     and shake the dust off your feet as a protest against
     them!'

6   So they set out, and went from village to village
     preaching the gospel and healing people everywhere.

7   All these things came to the ears of Herod the tetrarch
     and caused him acute anxiety, because some people were
     saying that John had risen from the dead,

8   some maintaining that the prophet Elijah had appeared,
     and others that one of the old-time prophets had come
     back.

9   'I beheaded John,' said Herod. 'Who can this be that I
     hear all these things about?'
     And he tried to find a way of seeing Jesus.

10   Then the apostles returned, and when they had made
     their report to Jesus of what they had done, he took
     them with him privately and retired into a town called
     Bethsaida.

In Jesus' instructions to his 'missionaries' we notice their
extraordinary defencelessness. They have literally nothing
but the clothes they stand up in, the power and authority
given them by Jesus and the job he has set them to do. That
is all: and that is the real and essential Christian.

Herod's cogitations fill up the time while the twelve are away. In their fumbling way they open the question of Jesus' identity and foreshadow the true declaration that Peter will soon make. We are also pointed towards the trial and death of Jesus, for it is only then that Herod's wish to see him will be fulfilled. Luke leaves out Mark's Salome story in the interests of keeping a clearer narrative line: it is so much a story-in-itself that it is easily detachable, something of a distraction, and without the gruesome interest that it had for Mark's martyr church.

After their mission the twelve return to the one who sent them out. Retirement and rest, in typical Lucan scene-change, follow their public work. Just as typically retirement is *into a town*, not a *desert place* as in Mark and Matthew.

9.11–17

11   But the crowds observed this and followed him. And he welcomed them and talked to them about the kingdom of God, and cured those who were in need of healing.

12   As the day drew to its close the twelve came to him and said,

'Please dismiss the crowd now so that they can go to the villages and farms round about and find some food and shelter, for we're quite in the wilds here.'

13   'You give them something to eat!' returned Jesus.

'But we've nothing here,' they replied, 'except five loaves and two fish, unless you want us to go and buy food for all this crowd?'

14   (There were approximately five thousand men there.)

Then Jesus said to the disciples,

'Get them to sit down in groups of about fifty.'

15   This they did, making them all sit down.

16   Then he took the five loaves and the two fish and looked up to Heaven, blessed them, broke them into pieces

and passed them to his disciples to serve to the crowd.
17 Everybody ate and was satisfied. Afterwards they collected twelve baskets full of broken pieces which were
left over.

The last passage told us nothing about how the twelve
fared on their mission, just that Jesus sent them, they went,
and they returned. But this story gives a telling and sharp
description of what it is like to be a follower of Christ in the
world.

The scene switches again: from privacy to public life. The
Christian is not only related to Christ but also to a world
crying out for healing and food; the crowd comes on to the
scene, and religious serenity is shattered. The twelve (Luke's
interest in the founding fathers) cannot cope out of their
own tiny resources, so *Please dismiss the crowd!* Jesus' reply
opposes their wish to make these people somebody else's
responsibility: *You give them something to eat.* The reluctance of
the twelve, reasonable in itself, is without faith, that eager
waiting upon the God who can make something out of
nothing. Not so with Jesus; he *looked up to Heaven* and in his
hands next to nothing becomes more than enough.

The story reads as a parable of Christian ministry to the
world. It seems likely that the early church treasured and
embellished it for this reason – it is in John, twice in Matthew
and Mark, and once here in Luke (six instances all together),
which shows it to have been a widespread and popular
tradition. The clue to the meaning of many stories is at the
end, and here the *twelve baskets* signify the twelve tribes of
Israel. The church is a new Israel, brought into being by
God's action through Christ and the disciples' obedience to
his command – but not out of their resourcefulness. Here is
bracing doctrinal comfort for timid Christians, comfort very
similar to that of the eucharist whose familiar pattern may
well have helped to shape this story. The twelve have no

more to offer than the crowd. They too are helpless. But they do what Jesus says and so become the means by which his fulfilment is given to others and a new human community begun.

9. 18–27

18 Then came this incident. While Jesus was praying by himself, having only the disciples near him, he asked them this question:

'Who are the crowd saying that I am?'

19 'Some say that you are John the Baptist,' they replied. 'Others that you are Elijah, and others think that one of the old-time prophets has come back to life.'

20 Then he said,

'And who do you say that I am?'

'God's Christ!' said Peter.

21 But Jesus expressly told them not to say a word to anybody,

22 at the same time warning them of the inevitability of the Son of Man's great suffering, of his repudiation by the elders, chief priests and scribes, and of his death and of being raised to life again on the third day.

23 Then he spoke to them all:

'If anyone wants to follow in my footsteps, he must give up all right to himself, carry his cross every day and keep close behind me.

24 For the man who wants to save his life will lose it, but the man who loses his life for my sake will save it.

25 For what is the use of a man gaining the whole world if he loses or forfeits his own soul?

26 If anyone is ashamed of me and my words, the Son of Man will be ashamed of him, when he comes in his glory and the glory of the Father and the holy angels.

27 I tell you the simple truth – there are men standing here

today who will not taste death until they have seen the
kingdom of God!'

We are getting into that mysterious centre of the gospel
in which Jesus and Christian discipleship will be shown in
paradoxical conjunctions of rejection and acceptance, suffering and glory, understanding and misunderstanding. If Luke
were a painstaking follower of Mark we should have to wait
longer before reaching this point. Instead, with a stroke bold
enough to alarm and perplex generations of cautious
scholars, he cuts Mark 6.45–8.26: – a very sizeable section. The
effect of this is (as usual) to make his gospel the most read-
able of all because of the greater tautness and grip of its
story-line. Luke feels it is time for his readers to be brought
to the crux. He is prepared to jettison the intervening
material in Mark as not containing anything indispensable
to his purposes, and one incident, the Gentile Syro-Phoe-
nician woman, which he would not want to use in this book.
Journeys into Gentile territory belong in Acts.

The first words are only in Luke (*While Jesus was praying by
himself, having only his disciples near him*). He sees Jesus as a man of
prayer, the activity which opens the world to new possibilities; and shows him as such at particularly solemn and
significant points. *Only the disciples* are *near him*: this too should
prepare us for a disclosure of the intimate secrets of the
gospel. In a few words Luke creates an expectant and devout
atmosphere which leads into the key question of who Jesus
is. The crowd think highly of him: a great religious figure.
But the disciples, through their spokesman Peter, recognize
him as something more final than that – *God's Christ*, the long-
awaited one whom God has anointed to be his regent. But
they are *not to say a word to anybody* – why? There is no one
answer to this, but a likely one is that such a recognition
can only come from faith. To make the thing public would
be to make it a matter of controversy or thoughtless and

over-enthusiastic acceptance, and not of faith at all. For some such reasons the demons were silenced when they recognized him. But more likely and more weighty in this instance is the answer suggested by the words spoken by Jesus which follow: a true evaluation cannot be made until the drama is complete, and that is not yet. The evangelist even leaves out the dramatic Marcan incident of Peter's remonstration and rebuke ('get thee behind me Satan'), possibly in order that this solemn teaching should not be interrupted, probably out of reverence for the apostle.

No sooner have the disciples acknowledged Jesus' majesty and pre-eminence than he points them, paradoxically but relentlessly, to something quite opposite – to suffering, disgrace and death and a new life on the other side of it. Before this in our gospel the title *Son of Man* has stood for power and glory. Now it is given a new and more disturbing shade of meaning which is immediately attached to Jesus' true followers as well as himself. *If anyone wants to follow in my footsteps, he must give up all right to himself, carry his cross every day and keep close behind me.* This sentence should be read as a whole. Christianity is not *just* self-denial. If it were it would be no different from repression. It is self-denial for a purpose, and that purpose is to take up (like Christ and unlike most people) the evil and disgrace in the world, to accept responsibility for it and carry it. In this way Christian forgetfulness of self is like that of any man engaged in some momentously significant enterprise or of a craftsman absorbed in his work – and not a neurosis. As such it is the disciple's daily and everyday discipline.

Verse 24 is the gospel in a nutshell: stern and tough, yet opening up the great possibility of finding oneself and more. The hardness and the joy of discipleship are contained in this universal maxim. But notice again that it is not just a matter of throwing things away in a fit of high-minded impatience. It is for a purpose, for a cause and for a person – *for my sake.* The following verses make this clear. The one crucial thing is to belong to Christ and not to be ashamed of it; then in the great day of the Son of Man's judgment he will not be ashamed of his own. Verse 27 certainly refers to the early Christians' expectation that that great day would be soon, but Luke with his more long-term view may well have understood the kingdom as becoming accessible in the establishment of the Christian community. At Acts 7.56 Stephen 'sees' that kingdom as a present reality.

9.28–36

28 About eight days after these sayings, Jesus took Peter, James and John and went off with them to the hillside to pray.

29 And then, while he was praying, the whole appearance of his face changed and his clothes became white and dazzling.

30 Suddenly two men could be seen talking with Jesus. They were Moses and Elijah –

31 revealed in heavenly splendour, and their talk was about the way he must take and the end he must fulfil in Jerusalem.

32 But Peter and his companions had been overcome by sleep and it was as they struggled into wakefulness that they saw the glory of Jesus and the two men standing with him.

33 Just as they were parting from him, Peter said to Jesus, 'Master, it is wonderful for us to be here! Let us put up three shelters – one for you, one for Moses and one for Elijah.' But he did not know what he was saying.

34 While he was still talking, a cloud overshadowed them and awe swept over them as it enveloped them.

35 A voice came out of the cloud, saying, 'This is my Son, my chosen! Listen to him!'

36   But when the voice had spoken, they found no one there but Jesus. The disciples were reduced to silence, and in those days never breathed a word to anyone of what they had seen.

Here, as in the baptism scene which showed Jesus as Messiah, we have a great tableau, an icon in which the gathered symbols all point to Jesus as a Messiah who must go through suffering. The structure is of diagrammatic clarity: a centre framed by points above, below and on each side, like a diamond. Jesus is in the centre, standing on 'the' mountain with its reminiscence of Sinai and Horeb. On one side of him are those whose stories foreshadow his own: Moses representing the Law, Elijah standing for the prophets. Together they embody the whole Old Testament witness and hope. From above comes the cloud (symbol of God's presence and glory in the book of Exodus – see Exodus 16.10, 24.15–18 particularly, and 40.38) and the divine voice. Below are the disciples, asleep at first and then awake and confused.

This fundamental symbolic-theological pattern Luke has inherited from Mark. He has added special touches of his own. For the sake of these, and in order to understand this central scene as well as possible, some more detailed comments will be useful.

About eight days after. Why should Luke say eight when Mark and Matthew both say six? Seven days is a full week. Six therefore suggests something short of fullness, but eight suggests a new 'week' altogether, i.e. for Luke a new phase in his story.

Peter, James and John are the inner group within the twelve, the seed of the Christian church, so they must be there for this revelation. There is no sense in trying to locate *the hillside* geographically. It is the mountain of God.

While he was praying. By now we are used to this as a signal that great things are about to happen. Jesus was praying at

his baptism, before choosing the twelve, and before Peter's
recognition of him. He will do so again in Gethsemane.
Here the praying carries on to the glorious change into
heavenly light.

The section from verse 31 (*revealed in heavenly splendour . . .*)
to the middle of verse 33 (*. . . parting from him*) is inserted
by Luke and not found elsewhere. *The way he must take
and the end he must fulfil* is literally in the Greek 'his Exodus
which he was going to fulfil'. With this one phrase Luke both
links the transfiguration to the cross and resurrection more
overtly than the other gospel-writers do and also characterizes the coming Easter events as being like the great Passover
deliverance which gave birth to the Jewish nation. *In Jerusalem*
is a signpost indicating that the circle of the gospel's geo-
graphical pattern is about to be closed. There we started and
there we shall end. We are now midway. The three disciples
are *overcome with sleep*, so very likely it is night – a time for
wonder and revelations in Luke. Further than that, the
disciples being asleep shows that it happens without them
and apart from them: they wake up to it. Peter then suggests
making *three shelters. . . . He did not know what he was saying* – but Luke
does! This is a continuation of the Exodus imagery which we
have seen in the mountain, the cloud and Moses, and which
has been brought into the open with the reference to Jesus'
impending Exodus. In the days of the journey to the
promised land the Jews lived in tents (tabernacles), and
among them was the tent of God (Exodus 36.8–19). In Jesus'
time this was remembered every year in the Feast of Tabernacles (Leviticus 23.42 and John 7.2), and it was believed that
in the last days when God's will had triumphed on earth
all the nations would come to this festival. So Peter is suggesting (unknowingly) that that time is now near.

The disciples fall under the great shadow of God's glory
(the cloud) and *awe swept over them* (Luke's characteristic motif
of fear at the divine presence) as they went into the cloud

(his addition). The disciples, like Moses (Exodus 24.18 is the source of this phrase), enter into full and mysterious communion with God. There, in that obliterating mist where there is nothing familiar or palpable, they hear the divine words which are the climax of the story and find *no one there but Jesus*. The founder-members of the church are taken into the heart of its mystery. The last sentence is Luke's. It underlines the awe-inspiring and unutterable solemnity of this vision of Jesus' nature and destiny, the central tableau and image of the focus of Christian experience.

9.37–43a

37 Then on the following day, as they came down the hillside, a great crowd met him.

38 Suddenly a man from the crowd shouted out, 'Master, please come and look at my son! He's my only child,

39 and without any warning some spirit gets hold of him and he calls out suddenly. Then it convulses him until he foams at the mouth, and only after a fearful struggle does it go away and leave him bruised all over.

40 I begged your disciples to get rid of it, but they couldn't.'

41 'You really are an unbelieving and difficult people,' replied Jesus. 'How long must I be with you, how long must I put up with you? Bring him here to me.'

42 But even while the boy was on his way, the spirit hurled him to the ground in a dreadful convulsion. Then Jesus reprimanded the evil spirit, healed the lad and handed him back to his father.

43 And everybody present was amazed at this demonstration of the power of God.

This story shows Jesus as an exorcist – a recognized and common calling in his time. The sources Luke uses are

Matthew and Mark, but as usual he adapts them to his own purposes. He agrees with Matthew in cutting out Mark's graphic detail about the disease. But whereas Matthew uses the story to develop his teaching about faith, Luke does two characteristic things: he humanizes it by adding that this is the father's *only child* and that Jesus, having cured him, *handed him back to his father*; he theologizes it by saying (through the crowd) that it is a *demonstration of the power* and majestic glory *of God*. In this way he gives an instance of that belonging-together of humanity and heavenly splendour which he introduced in his Christmas stories.

9.43b–50

And while everybody was full of wonder at all the things they saw him do, Jesus was saying to the disciples,

44   'Store up in your minds what I tell you nowadays, for the Son of Man is going to be handed over to the power of men.'

45   But they made no sense of this saying – something made it impossible for them to understand it, and they were afraid to ask him what he meant.

46   Then an argument arose among them as to who should be the greatest.

47   But Jesus, knowing what they were arguing about, picked up a little child and stood him by his side.

48   And then he said to them,

'Anyone who accepts a little child in my name is accepting me, and the man who accepts me is accepting the one who sent me. It is the humblest among you all who is really the greatest.'

49   Then John broke in,

'Master, we saw a man driving out evil spirits in your name, but we stopped him, for he is not one of us who follow you.'

50   But Jesus told him,
     'You must not stop him. The man who is not against
     you is on your side.'

The sense of momentous crisis in this central section has
been built up by a series of switches in the atmosphere –
rapid 'cutting' in cinematic terms. The glory of the transfiguration was followed by the distress of the possessed boy.
No sooner is that resolved by a demonstration of God's
power and majesty than the shadow of death falls on Jesus.
But this, instead of sparking off histrionic opposition, brings
an exhortation to an extraordinary gentleness and acceptance
centred on the figures of the child and the non-party member. The lack of understanding between Jesus and his
followers gives an extra twist to the tension.

Verse 44 shows the paradox of a powerful figure (Son of
Man) who is at the mercy of his enemies. The disciples'
failure to understand springs from some kind of 'mental
block' and from fear.

Their stupidity comes into the open when they express
the ordinary human status-obsession: *who should be the greatest?*
Jesus' answer is, as always, to up-end worldly values. The
smallest is the greatest, and only in accepting the little things
do we receive the big thing which is God, *the one who sent me.*
John's demonstration of party spirit – another bid for
security – is met in the same way. *In your name* does not just
mean 'under the Christian label', for the name in the Bible
stands for work and power, the reality of a thing and not
just its category.

6

Towards the Ambiguous City

9.51–62

51   Now as the days before he should be taken into Heaven were running out,

52 he set his face firmly towards Jerusalem, and sent messengers ahead of him. They set out and entered a Samaritan village to make preparations for him.

53 But the people there refused to welcome him because he was obviously intending to go to Jerusalem.

54 When the disciples James and John saw this, they said,
   'Master, do you want us to call down fire from Heaven and burn them all up?'

55   But Jesus turned and reproved them,

56 and they all went on to another village.

57   As the little company made its way along the road, a man said to him,
   'I'm going to follow you wherever you go.'

58   And Jesus replied,
   'Foxes have earths, birds have nests, but the Son of Man has nowhere to lay his head.'

59   But he said to another man,
   'Follow me.'
   And he replied,
   'Let me go and bury my father first.'

60   But Jesus told him,
   'Leave the dead to bury their own dead. You must come away and preach the kingdom of God.'

61   Another man said to him,

'I am going to follow you, Lord, but first let me bid
farewell to my people at home.'

62   But Jesus told him,
        'Anyone who puts his hand to the plough and then
looks behind him is useless for the kingdom of God.'

We have reached an ominous point in the gospel from
which Luke peers forward to its end – which will in turn be
the turning-point between the gospel and Acts: Jesus' being
taken into Heaven. We already know the importance Luke
attaches to his time-scale. Here he emphasizes it solemnly
and portentously, *the days . . . were running out*. Jesus *set his face . . .
towards* Jerusalem, a phrase which elsewhere in the Bible has
a menacing ring to it (Jeremiah 21.10, Ezekiel 6.2). The
threat here has two directions: Jesus is going to prophesy
against Jerusalem and denounce it (13.34,35 and Chapter 19),
and he is going to die there. The glorious City of God in
which the story began takes on the sinister aspect of the City
of Destruction, an ambiguity which will stick to it from now
on. The sending of the messengers suggests something of the
dignity of a royal progress. The four incidents which follow,
each as brief as one frame in a strip cartoon, point up a new
urgency appropriate to the new turn in events and direction.
        The first is Luke's own. He has sympathy for the Samaritans
although they had been on consistently bad terms with the
Jerusalem Jews ever since the Exile to Babylon, when they
had stayed behind. Although both worshipped the same
God, or even because of it, their relations were no better
than those of Catholics and Protestants in Ulster. The
Samaritan suspicion of Jerusalem-bound travellers is thus as
deep-seated as James' and John's reaction is natural. Jesus
blocks it with a compassion which is characteristic of him in
this gospel. The destroying *fire from heaven* is a reference to
Elijah's ferocious behaviour in 2 Kings 1.10 ff. But whereas
previously in this gospel, and particularly in the Nain story,

Jesus has been likened to Elijah, now he is seen in direct contrast to him. An era has begun in which the newness of Christianity is more distinct. But Jesus does not enter the Samaritan village: the gospel will come to Samaria in Acts, not now.

The three stories about discipleship are little more than graphic illustrations. The first two are also in Matthew and speak for themselves. Following Jesus means being uprooted from normal security because *preaching the kingdom of God* (Luke's addition to his source) overrides even the most pious natural obligations. The last illustration tells of a new departure which must never be gone back on or regretted (cf. 17.32). It also makes a further contrast with Elijah who allowed Elisha to say good-bye to his parents after he had called him (1 Kings 19.19 ff.). Even that slight delay is now out of the question.

10. 1–16

1　　Later on the Lord commissioned seventy other disciples and sent them off in twos as advance-parties into every town and district where he intended to go himself.

2　　'There is a great harvest,' he told them, 'but only a few are working in it – which means you must pray to the Lord of the harvest that he will send out more reapers to bring in his harvest.

3　　'Now go on your way. I am sending you out like lambs among wolves.

4　　Don't carry a purse or a bag or a pair of shoes, and don't stop to greet anyone you meet on the road.

5　　When you go into a house, say first of all, "Peace be to this household!"

6　　If there is a lover of peace there, he will accept your words of blessing, and if not, they will come back to you.

7 Stay in the same house and eat and drink whatever they put before you – a workman deserves his wages. But don't move from one house to another.

8   'Whatever town you go into and the people welcome you, eat the meals they give you

9 and heal the people who are ill there. Tell them, "The kingdom of God is very near to you now."

10 But whenever you come into a town and they will not welcome you, you must go into the streets and say,

11 "We brush off even the dust of your town from our feet as a protest against you. But it is still true that the kingdom of God has arrived!"

12 I assure you that it will be easier for Sodom in "that day" than for that town.

13   'Alas for you, Chorazin, and alas for you, Bethsaida! For if Tyre and Sidon had seen the demonstrations of God's power that you have seen, they would have repented long ago in sackcloth and ashes.

14 It will be easier for Tyre and Sidon in the judgment than for you!

15 As for you, Capernaum, do you think you will be exalted to the heavens? I tell you you will go hurtling down among the dead!'

   Then he added to the seventy,

16   'Whoever listens to you is listening to me, and the man who rejects you rejects me too. And the man who rejects me rejects the One who sent me!'

The long and unified section which begins here and ends at 10.24 (though we shall deal with it in two parts) matches the sending of the twelve at 9.1–6 and 9.10. The mission of the church is to emerge as the major theme of Acts. Here its two prototypes frame, or bracket, the axis of the gospel: transfiguration and departure for Jerusalem (see p. 99). But there is also contrast. The mission of the seventy is a much

bigger thing than the mission of the twelve. Jesus has much
more to say about it, both by way of preparation and in
celebration of its success. The number seventy is more far-
reaching than twelve, the number of the tribes of Israel. It
refers to the seventy nations of the world in Genesis 10.
Things have moved a long way since the beginning of
Chapter 9. A new impetus is at work, the secret of which
lies in the intervening material.

Luke has taken a lot of trouble over the mission charge,
stitching together pieces from chapters 10 and 11 of Matthew
and adding a bit of his own in verses 7–9 which read like a
little practical guide to etiquette and tactics for Christian
missionaries. His great and particular contribution to the
whole matter is typical. He breaks Matthew 11.21–27 at the
division of verses 24 and 25 and inserts the return of the
missionaries (verses 17–20) in the gap he has made. In other
words, he adapts the kind of long oration characteristic of
Matthew into a dramatic narrative characteristic of himself:
something happens, it becomes a story.

Urgency is still the dominating note as the discipleship
which was called for in the previous section moves into
action. The two references to *the kingdom of God* (verses 9 and
11) are peculiar to Luke and are for him the point of the
whole enterprise. The fact that God is in charge becomes
immediate and present to people in the proclamation of the
advance-parties of the kingdom, the reapers of the great
harvest of the day of the Lord ('Put in the sickle, for the
harvest is ripe', Joel 3.13, cf. Revelation 14.18). It is all happening now rather than in a remote visionary future, and as far
as the hearers are concerned it can go two ways: peace,
blessing and healing if they accept the message, or rejection
and destruction if they do not. Being Jewish is no protection
(verses 13–15). Repentance, which means a change of heart
and mind rather than feelings of guilt, is the only qualifi-
cation. Reaction to the message of the advance-parties is

nothing less than reaction to the God who is driving it all.

10.17–24

17   Later the seventy came back full of joy.

'Lord,' they said, 'even evil spirits obey us when we use your name!'

18   'Yes,' returned Jesus, 'I was watching and saw Satan fall from Heaven like a flash of lightning!

19   It is true that I have given you the power to tread on snakes and scorpions and to overcome all the enemy's power – there is nothing at all that can do you any harm.

20   Yet it is not your power over evil spirits which should give such joy, but the fact that your names are written in Heaven.'

21   At that moment Jesus' heart was filled with joy by the Holy Spirit, and he exclaimed,

'O Father, Lord of Heaven and earth, I thank you for hiding these things from the wise and the clever and for showing them to mere children! Yes, I thank you, Father, that this was your will.' Then he went on,

22   'Everything has been put in my hands by my Father; and nobody knows who the Son is except the Father. Nobody knows who the Father is except the Son – and the man to whom the Son chooses to reveal him!'

23   Then he turned to his disciples and said to them quietly,

'How fortunate you are to see what you are seeing!

24   I tell you that many prophets and kings have wanted to see what you are seeing but they never saw it, and to hear what you are hearing but they never heard it.'

The first half of the passage is Luke's own (verses 17–21a). The second half is also in Matthew (verses 21b–24). There is thus more emphasis on this incident in Luke than in any other gospel, which is characteristic of the man who is going to write the great missionary saga of Acts. His narrative skill is seen in such a weaving together and overlapping of themes as this which reminds readers of Simeon's prophecy in the past and glimpses the great movements of the future. The overall structure is a crescendo, leading up to the incantatory theology of verse 22 and the exultant blessing, or congratulation, of verses 23 and 24. A few remarks about details may help to point up the excitement and happiness which run through this passage.

Evil spirits were malign spiritual parasites, stronger than men obviously; but weaker than God. So if Jesus' name (i.e. his power made present through his name) can subdue them, who is he? Verse 22 gives the answer in the form of a credal-poetic statement which we can imagine as being familiar in the Christian church. The astounding vision of Satan falling from Heaven is paralleled at Revelation 12.8,9. It is an apocalyptic theme, an image of the final triumph of God over evil. Satan embodies everything that thwarts the divine will of peace on earth amongst men. The apocalyptic image of the harvest appeared earlier at verse 2. Psalm 91 is a source for verse 19. Verse 20 cautions the Christian not to see himself as a magic man but rather as, by God's grace, an heir to Heaven. Luke adds the note about Jesus' joy. It is in the Holy Spirit, which is the opposite of Satan and the initiator and driving power of God's purposes, as in the birth stories. He also adds the first half of verse 23 as a reminder of the narrative line in the middle of an exalted oration and to put further emphasis on the disciples. It is similar to the famous 22.61. The remaining words, isolated and given importance by this short introduction, proclaim Luke's great theme of the fulfilment of the Old Testament and of all human hopes at this point in the course of time: the coming of Christ and the sending of his disciples.

GENERAL NOTE

Luke has now turned the axis of his story and pointed it in a new direction: towards Jerusalem. Having done this in 9.51–10.24, he can take time in the next eight chapters to give us a wealth of teaching with little definite narrative connection. The drive and excitement generated in the preceding section with all its emphasis on the time now allow him to free-wheel as far as this theme is concerned. It carries him through – just! The teaching in Matthew's gospel, along with didactic material of his own, supply all he needs.

10.25–37

25 Once one of the experts in the Law stood up to test him and said,
'Master, what must I do to be sure of eternal life?'

26 'What does the Law say and what has your reading taught you?' said Jesus.

27 'The Law says, "Thou shalt love the Lord thy God with all thy heart and with all thy soul and with all thy strength and with all thy mind – and thy neighbour as thyself",' he replied.

28 'Quite right,' said Jesus. 'Do that and you will live.'

29 But the man, wanting to justify himself, continued, 'But who is my "neighbour"?'

30 And Jesus gave him the following reply:
'A man was once on his way down from Jerusalem to Jericho. He fell into the hands of bandits who stripped off his clothes, beat him up, and left him half dead.

31 It so happened that a priest was going down that road, and when he saw him, he passed by on the other side.

32 A Levite also came on the scene and when he saw him, he too passed by on the other side.

33 But then a Samaritan traveller came along to the place where the man was lying, and at the sight of him he was touched with pity.

34 He went across to him and bandaged his wounds, pouring on oil and wine. Then he put him on his own mule, brought him to an inn and did what he could for him.

35 Next day he took out two silver coins and gave them to the inn-keeper with the words, "Look after him, will you? I will pay you back whatever more you spend, when I come through here on my return."

36 Which of these three seems to you to have been a neighbour to the bandits' victim?'

37 'The man who gave him practical sympathy,' he replied.
    'Then you go and give the same,' returned Jesus.

The tale of the Good Samaritan is so well known and speaks for itself so unmistakably that it needs little other comment than Jesus' final injunction. It occurs only in Luke and has many of his trade-marks: its length, the highly-finished Greek of the original, the theme of a journey with a turning-point, the prominence of the Samaritan as a figure from the fringe of orthodox Judaism, the human sympathy which informs it all. But no one's creative imagination starts from nowhere. Verses 25–27, adapted from Matthew 22.34–38, which are themselves an adaptation of Mark 12.28, are Luke's jumping-off point. But Luke knows that we need to see it happen if it is really to sink in, so doctrine becomes story. That is *the* Lucan trade-mark. The question at the outset, *who is my neighbour?* differs from the one at the end, *which of these three seems to you to have been a neighbour?* so either the tale existed in some form before it was included in the gospel, or it has turned the question round from the theoretical 'who is my neighbour?' to the practical 'who should I be neighbourly to?' Notice that, like the Prodigal Son and the Crafty Steward, this is a secular story. The Samaritan's motivation is not pious in a religious sense. The kingdom of God is seen in worldly happenings. (2 Chronicles 28.14f. is an Old Testament source.)

10.38–11.13

38 As they continued their journey, Jesus came to a village and a woman called Martha welcomed him to her house.

39 She had a sister by the name of Mary who settled down at the Lord's feet and was listening to what he said.

40 But Martha was very worried about her elaborate preparations and she burst in, saying,

'Lord, don't you mind that my sister has left me to do everything by myself? Tell her to get up and help me!'

41 But the Lord answered her,

'Martha, my dear, you are worried and bothered about providing so many things.

42 Only one thing is really needed. Mary has chosen the best part and it must not be taken away from her!'

1 One day it happened that Jesus was praying in a certain place, and after he had finished, one of his disciples said,

'Lord, teach us how to pray, as John used to teach his disciples.'

2 'When you pray,' returned Jesus, 'you should say, "Father, may your name be honoured – may your kingdom come.

3 Give us the bread we need for each day,

4 and forgive us our failures, for we forgive everyone who fails us; and keep us clear of temptation."'

5 Then he added,

'If any of you has a friend, and goes to him in the

middle of the night and says, "Lend me three loaves, my dear fellow,

6 for a friend of mine has just arrived after a journey and I have no food to put in front of him";

7 and then he answers from inside the house, "Don't bother me with your troubles. The front door is locked and my children and I have gone to bed. I simply cannot get up now and give you anything!"

8 Yet, I tell you, that even if he won't get up and give him what he wants simply because he is his friend, yet if he persists, he will rouse himself and give him everything he needs.

9 And so I tell you, ask and it will be given you, search and you will find, knock and the door will be opened to you.

10 The one who asks will always receive; the one who is searching will always find, and the door is opened to the man who knocks.

11 Some of you are fathers, and if your son asks you for some fish, would you give him a snake instead,

12 or if he asks you for an egg, would you make him a present of a scorpion?

13 So, if you, for all your evil, know how to give good things to your children, how much more likely is it that your Heavenly Father will give the Holy Spirit to those who ask him!'

We turn from doing to listening and asking – a characteristic switch. Prayer as a connection between Heaven and earth is a particular interest of Luke's (cf. 5.33). It is a connection which comes about in the passivity of our listening to God (like Mary) and in our asking God for what we want (like the persistent friend). It is letting God affect us and our seeking to affect him. Both sides are there in the prayer which stands between the two illustrative stories. Its first half is an opening-up to God, its second an asking of him to fulfil our needs.

The two stories are only in Luke. They take the place of the directions in Matthew 6.1–8 and have, typically, a more human and less overtly religious character. Just as typically they are vivid anecdotes rather than rules. The prayer is also in Matthew in a longer version. Verses 9–13 are virtually the same as Matthew 7.7–11 except for the substitution of 'Holy Spirit' for 'good things', since it includes, supports and initiates all good things.

The only other appearance of Martha and Mary is in John 11, which is a different story. Luke uses them as a contrast of two types. He has noticed that resentment and lurking crossness which beset the busy person and which the distractions of activity cannot dispel. Mary, on the other hand, is sufficiently relaxed to listen, and so recalls the other Mary at the annunciation. J. B. Phillips' *what he said* is a paraphrase for Luke's 'his word' which is a precise term for the gospel message (cf. 1.2), though it does not have the philosophical range of John's use of the word.

The prayer is introduced by a glimpse of Jesus praying and the disciples' request to him to teach them how to do it both peculiar to Luke. This version is shorter and simpler than Matthew's which has led many scholars to consider it older, although abbreviation is just as possible as accretion with the passage of time. But if Luke is abbreviating Matthew, it is hard to see why he left out 'Thy will be done' and 'deliver us from evil'. One can only say that the two versions are different. The prayer is not distinctively Christian at any point and could just as well be used by Jews. It amounts to a petition to God to be himself, now and in the future, and to give us our two indispensable needs, bread and forgiveness. Temptation does not refer to minor naughtiness but to the terrible experience of being under the sort of test and trial which could break us.

The illustration of the importunate friend shows prayer as petition in an outright and uninhibited sense, paralleled only by the importunate widow at 18.1–8. Very likely it was suggested to Luke by the petition *give us the bread we need*. We do not need it only for ourselves but for the people who come to us. Delicate and rational souls are often offended by the notion of petitionary prayer. The graphic humour of this parable (cf. the sharp-practising steward at 16.1–9) will be unwelcome to them. But Luke believes that the gospel is for those who know they need it (cf. 5.31) and ask for it. Unabashed asking is of the essence of faith for him, so he is not inclined to water it down. Rather, in the last verses, he drives it home. If ordinary life with all its shortcomings is sustained by asking and receiving, how much more the fuller life of the disciple whose requests will be fulfilled by nothing less than the Holy Spirit, the active presence of God.

11.14–54. GENERAL NOTE

Here is another abrupt change of tone and scene: from private teaching to public argument which carries on until the end of the chapter. Most of the material for chapter 11 Luke shares with Matthew or takes from him, but up to verse 37 he widens the scope by omitting Matthew's references to the Pharisees as the butt of Jesus' teaching. It is for everyone. From verse 37 onwards they are the target, though giving way to their colleagues the lawyers at verse 45 (Luke's insertion). In verses 53 and 54 Luke adds a note on the crafty hostility of Jesus' enemies which springs from his preceding attacks on them and so tightens the tension.

11.14–23

14 Another time, Jesus was expelling an evil spirit which was preventing a man from speaking, and as soon as the

evil spirit left him, the dumb man found his speech, to the amazement of the crowds.

15 But some of them said,

'He expels these spirits because he is in league with Beelzebub, the chief of the evil spirits.'

16 Others among them, to test him, tried to get a sign from Heaven out of him.

17 But he knew what they were thinking and told them,

'Any kingdom divided against itself is doomed and a disunited household will collapse.

18 And if Satan disagrees with Satan, how does his kingdom continue? – for I know you are saying that I expel evil spirits because I am in league with Beelzebub.

19 But if I do expel devils because I am an ally of Beelzebub, who is your own sons' ally when they do the same thing? They can settle that question for you.

20 But if it is by the finger of God that I am expelling evil spirits, then the kingdom of God has swept over you here and now.

21 'When a strong man armed to the teeth guards his own house, his property is secure.

22 But when a stronger man comes and conquers him, he removes all the arms on which he pinned his faith and divides the spoil among his friends.

23 'Anyone who is not with me is against me, and the man who does not gather with me is really scattering.

Luke is closer to Matthew's version of this argument than to Mark's, though he puts aside the saying about the sin against the Holy Spirit for use later and brings in the request for a sign earlier (verse 16). He feels free to adapt his sources. His first most notable contribution in this passage is to substitute *the finger of God* for 'the Spirit of God'. This recalls an older dispute, the confrontation of Moses the wonder-working servant of God with the Egyptian magicians at

Exodus 8.19. But those opponents recognized what was going on and these ones do not – an unflattering comparison! The capacity to see what is going on is, typically, the crux of the story. Refusal to do so, here as elsewhere, leads to absurdity and the confusion of right and wrong. Jesus' appeal is to sheer clarity and common sense. Fear and prejudice make the muddle. Luke's second contribution to this account is in verses 21 and 22, which expand and emphasize the picture of the strong man in Mark and Matthew. Jesus is more powerful than the strongest forces of evil. He is the conquering Christ of Easter Day – see Colossians 2.15 for a grander version of the same image.

11.24–32

24   'When the evil spirit comes out of a man, it wanders through waterless places looking for rest, and when it fails to find any, it says, "I will go back to my house from which I came."

25   When it arrives, it finds it cleaned and all in order.

26   Then it goes and collects seven other spirits more evil than itself to keep it company, and they all go in and make themselves at home. The last state of that man is worse than the first.'

27   And while he was still saying this, a woman in the crowd called out and said,

   'Oh, what a blessing for a woman to have brought you into the world and nursed you!'

28   But Jesus replied,

   'Yes, but a far greater blessing is to hear the word of God and obey it.'

29   Then as the people crowded closely around him, he continued,

   'This is an evil generation! It looks for a sign and it will be given no sign except that of Jonah.

30 Just as Jonah was a sign to the people of Nineveh, so will
    the Son of Man be a sign to this generation.
31 When the judgment comes, the Queen of the South will
    rise up with the men of this generation and she will
    condemn them. For she came from the ends of the
    earth to listen to the wisdom of Solomon, and there is
    more than the wisdom of Solomon with you now.
32 The men of Nineveh will stand up at the judgment with
    this generation and will condemn it. For they did repent
    when Jonah preached to them, and there is something
    more than Jonah's preaching with you now.'

Jesus attacks the things which spoil and block our ability
to live to the full: emptiness, sentimentality, and the stub-
born cynicism which refuses to attend to anything except
the stupendous.

Luke has linked Matthew's parable of the empty house to
the preceding passage about the prince of the devils. The
house is a man, left empty after the evil spirit has been driven
out of him. But evil spirits are parasites which cannot survive
without a host, so after brief wanderings it returns. Presumably the emptiness, cleanliness and attractive decoration
which he then finds suggest to him the idea of a party with
his friends, in which hell breaks loose. A cure is therefore
not just turning things out, but a new life with a new content.

The hard words to the gushingly enthusiastic woman are
a reminder of 8.19–21 about Jesus' true family. Over and
above such ties, real life is active response to God's word, by
which is meant the gospel of Jesus and the church.

But apparently people expect something more spectacular
than that. The *sign of Jonah* was nothing more than a solitary
man trying to wake people up to the divine judgment
hanging over them (though Matthew 12.40 gives, characteristically, a more esoterically Christian interpretation). Jesus
is like Jonah, only more so. In the *Queen of the South* (i.e. the

Queen of Sheba) we have a Gentile from an Old Testament story who listened attentively to the inspired wisdom of King Solomon. Both she and the Ninevites were Gentiles. The passage comes from St Matthew's gospel which is favourable to the Gentile mission. Luke is careful to keep Gentiles off the scene until Acts, but these two from the past can be admitted as signs and examples.

11.33–44

33   'No one takes a lamp and puts it in a cupboard or under a bucket, but on a lamp-stand, so that those who come in can see the light.

34   The lamp of your body is your eye. When your eye is sound, your whole body is full of light, but when your eye is evil, your whole body is full of darkness.

35   So be very careful that your light never becomes darkness.

36   For if your whole body is full of light, with no part of it in shadow, it will all be radiant – it will be like having a bright lamp to give you light.'

37   While he was talking, a Pharisee invited him to dinner. So he went into his house and sat down at table.

38   The Pharisee noticed with some surprise that he did not wash before the meal.

39   But the Lord said to him,
    'You Pharisees are fond of cleaning the outside of your cups and dishes, but inside yourselves you are full of greed and wickedness!

40   Have you no sense? Don't you realize that the one who made the outside is the maker of the inside as well?

41   If you would only make the inside clean by giving the contents to those in need, the outside becomes clean as a matter of course!

42   But alas for you Pharisees, for you pay out your tithe of mint and rue and every little herb, and lose sight of the

justice and the love of God. Yet these are the things you ought to have been concerned with – it need not mean leaving the lesser duties undone.

43 Yes, alas for you Pharisees, who love the front seats in the synagogues and having men bow down to you in public!

44 Alas for you, for you are like unmarked graves – men walk over your corruption without ever knowing it is there.'

The saying about light is a repeat of 8.16, with development from Matthew 6.22f. and from Luke's own pen. It makes a bridge between the preceding debate and what is to follow. The ability to see is the only necessary thing. It is a sickness of the eye that hinders Jesus' enemies. The doors of their perception need to be cleansed.

From here Luke goes on to use anti-Pharisaical material from Matthew 23. In verses 37 and 38 he characteristically provides a setting in life to relieve the long stretch of teaching with a touch of narrative. It is one of his favourite scenes, the dinner table. He adapts Matthew's version to make it clearer that the outside and inside of human life is the issue here rather than matters of ritual. God is concerned with content. Verse 41 reads literally 'give for alms those things which are within'. Doing good to others is not an external matter but consists in the giving of one's inmost self.

The rest of the passage is in the form of three curses on the Pharisees which, together with the subsequent three curses on the lawyers, are adapted from Matthew's seven curses in chapter 23. The first attacks their obsession with detail to the exclusion of what really matters: *justice* and (Luke's addition) *the love of God*. The second is aimed at their ridiculous self-importance and hunger for popular recognition, a perennial ecclesiastical vice. The third brings in a macabre note: having to do with such people is like walking over an unmarked grave, coming near death and defilement without knowing it.

11.45–54

45   Then one of the experts in the Law said to him,
     'Master, when you say things like this, you are insulting us as well.'

46   And he returned,
     'Yes, and I do blame you experts in the Law! For you pile up back-breaking burdens for men to bear, but you yourselves will not raise a finger to lift them.

47   Alas for you, for you build memorial tombs for the prophets – the very men whom your fathers murdered.

48   You show clearly enough how you approve your fathers' actions. They did the killing and you put up the memorials.

49   That is why the Wisdom of God has said, "I will send them prophets and apostles; some they will kill and some they will persecute!"

50   So that the blood of all the prophets shed from the foundation of the earth,

51   from Abel to Zachariah who died between the altar and the sanctuary, shall be charged to this generation. Yes, I tell you this generation must answer for it all!

52   'Alas for you experts in the Law, for you have taken away the key of knowledge. You have never gone in yourselves and you have hindered everyone else who was at the door!'

53   And when he left that place, the scribes and the Pharisees began to nurture a bitter hatred against him, and tried to draw him out on a great many subjects,

54   waiting to pounce on some incriminating remark.

The change of target which Luke makes here, lawyers

instead of Pharisees, has little significance but shows his inclination to break up the long Matthean discourse with touches of narrative. The moral authorities and guardians come in for three curses, none of which is out of date. The rigorousness which comes easily to the respectable and timid but falls hard on the others, the reverence paid by the establishment to characters it would never have tolerated in their lifetime, the dog-in-the-manger attitude of those who have excluded themselves from real life: all these are familiar enough. Zachariah could be the man who, according to Josephus, was killed in the Temple by guerrillas in A.D. 68, or he could be the martyred prophet in 2 Chronicles 24.20–22. Small changes made by Luke in Matthew's text include: *Wisdom of God* which is typical of Luke's liberal Judaism, and *taken away the key of knowledge* instead of 'shut the kingdom of Heaven', which has the same tendency. Luke is writing for a more general literary public than Matthew so uses terms which they will understand more easily than Matthew's technicalities.

Verses 53 and 54, which add a menacing note of drama, are Luke's addition.

12. I–12

1   Meanwhile, the crowds had gathered in thousands, so that they were actually treading on each other's toes, and Jesus, speaking primarily to his disciples, said,

'Be on your guard against yeast – I mean the yeast of the Pharisees, which is sheer pretence.

2   For there is nothing covered up which is not going to be exposed, nor anything private which is not going to be made public.

3   Whatever you may say in the dark will be heard in daylight, and whatever you whisper within four walls will be shouted from the house-tops.

4   'I tell you, as friends of mine, that you are not to be

afraid of those who can kill the body, but afterwards cannot do anything more.

5 I will show you the only one you need to fear – the one who, after he has killed, has the power to throw you into destruction! Yes, I tell you, it is right to stand in awe of him.

6 The market-price of five sparrows is two farthings, isn't it? Yet not one of them is forgotten in God's sight.

7 Why, the very hairs of your heads are all numbered! Don't be afraid then; you are worth more than a great many sparrows!

8 I tell you that every man who acknowledges me before men, I, the Son of Man, will acknowledge in the presence of the angels of God.

9 But the man who disowns me before men will find himself disowned before the angels of God!

10 'Anyone who speaks against the Son of Man will be forgiven, but there is no forgiveness for the man who speaks evil against the Holy Spirit.

11 And when they bring you before the synagogues and magistrates and authorities, don't worry as to what defence you are going to put up or what words you are going to use.

12 For the Holy Spirit will tell you at the time what is the right thing for you to say.'

Luke turns from Matthew 24 which attacks the Jewish authorities to Matthew 10 which is addressed to the disciples. He keeps the disciples, i.e. the Christians, as the primary audience for what follows, but the presence of a crowd of thousands hints at a much wider public. The authorities have been attacked for their covering up. This must be avoided like the plague; first because it spreads and grows like yeast, second because 'murder will out' and in the end there are no secrets.

The following verses reassure the disciples that God alone
matters. He will keep them. The only terror is to fall away
from him. His care for his own is graphically portrayed in
the images of sparrows and hairs. The Son of Man is the God-
appointed man from Heaven of Daniel who will judge all
men. Verses 8–10 show a distinction between Jesus and this
mythical figure, but the message is that holding fast to Jesus
is the only necessity. Verse 10 does not follow easily. Possibly
it means that the ultimate issue is not whether a man is a
Christian or not but whether he obeys such divine inspiration
as comes to him. Verses 11 and 12 are linked on by the theme
of the Spirit. Luke adapts the Matthean material to point
forward to the trials in Acts in which the faith and integrity
of the disciples will be put to the test.

12. 13–34

13   Then someone out of the crowd said to him,
    'Master, tell my brother to share his legacy with me.'

14   But Jesus replied,
    'My dear man, who appointed me a judge or arbitrator
in your affairs?'

15   And then, turning to the disciples, he said to them,
    'Notice that, and be on your guard against covetous-
ness in any shape or form. For a man's real life in no way
depends upon the number of his possessions.'

16   Then he gave them a parable in these words,
    'Once upon a time a rich man's farmland produced
heavy crops.

17   So he said to himself, "What shall I do, for I have no
room to store this harvest of mine?"

18   Then he said, "I know what I'll do. I'll pull down my
barns and build bigger ones where I can store all my
grain and my goods

19   and I can say to my soul, Soul, you have plenty of good

things stored up there for years to come. Relax! Eat,
drink and have a good time!"

20 But God said to him, "You fool, this very night you will
be asked for *your soul*! Then, who is going to possess all
that you have prepared?"

21 That is what happens to the man who hoards things for
himself and is not rich in the eyes of God.'

22 And then he added to the disciples,
'That is why I tell you, don't worry about life, wondering what you are going to eat, or what clothes your body
will need.

23 Life is much more important than food, and the body
more important than clothes.

24 Think of the ravens. They neither sow nor reap, and
they have neither store nor barn, but God feeds them.
And how much more valuable do you think you are
than birds?

25 Can any of you make himself even a few inches taller
however much he worries about it?

26 And if you can't manage a little thing like this, why do
you worry about anything else?

27 Think of the wild flowers, and how they neither work
nor weave. Yet I tell you that Solomon in all his glory
was never arrayed like one of these.

28 If God so clothes the grass, which flowers in the
field today and is burnt in the stove tomorrow, is
he not much more likely to clothe you, you little-
faiths?

29 You must not set your heart on what you eat or drink,
nor must you live in a state of anxiety.

30 The whole heathen world is busy about getting food
and drink, and your Father knows well enough that you
need such things.

31 No, set your heart on his kingdom, and your food and
drink will come as a matter of course.

32 Don't be afraid, you tiny flock! Your Father plans to give you the kingdom.

33 Sell your possessions and give the money away to those in need. Get yourselves purses that never grow old, inexhaustible treasure in Heaven, where no thief can ever reach it, or moth destroy it.

34 For wherever your treasure is, you may be certain that your heart will be there too!'

A feature of the gospel material peculiar to Luke is its numerous well-to-do characters. The Good Samaritan had money to spare, the father of the Prodigal Son was a man of substance, Zacchaeus is more rich than honest, the rich man who ignored Lazarus is ostentatiously affluent, the women of 8.2,3 look after Jesus from their own resources. This indicates a literate and comfortable bourgeoisie as Luke's readership. They are much in mind in this passage. The curses on the Pharisees and lawyers probably fell sweetly on their ears. Now the judgment comes nearer home as the perils of their own comfortable existence become the object of sharp warnings. Luke prefaces the Matthean material exhorting the disciples to trust in God's care with two stories of his own about covetousness and material security. This gives the subsequent teaching more concern with financial worries than discipleship.

In the first incident Jesus refuses to be used as an arbiter of a legal problem because greed lies behind the request. Paul shows a similar impatience with litigious Christians in I Corinthians 6.1–8.

The parable has something of the character of a traditional folk story on the perennial theme of the transience of worldly goods, but the opulent setting, interior dialogue and appeal to sheer sense of its present form are Lucan characteristics. It has a universal rather than a specifically Christian message – though verse 21 gives a religious twist.

The crisis, however, is not the Last Day of Jewish-Christian doctrine but death. The main part of the parable is the man's self-communings, a typically Lucan touch (cf. the Steward, chapter 16). They show a sublime complacency and a certain reasonableness. But the man has forgotten about God and his unpredictable ways. So for all his business sense (verse 18) he is a fool; a fool in the Bible being anyone who fails to take God into account (Psalms 73.22, 53.1, 2 Corinthians 11.23 etc.). Verse 21 provides a bridge to the Matthean material.

This is not much altered, except for the insertion of verses 26 and 33a. Matthew's 'birds' become *ravens*. The whole section puts right the follies in the preceding stories. A real life goes for the real thing. The rest follows. Verse 32 fills a gap in Matthew's version, assuring the disciples that the kingdom which they must seek will be theirs. Verses 33 and 34 give the incentive for such a life. Luke has nothing in common with those nice-minded Christians who balk at the idea of rewards.

12.35-48

35 'You must be ready dressed and have your lamps alight,

36 like men who wait to welcome their lord and master on his return from the wedding-feast, so that when he comes and knocks at the door, they may open it for him at once.

37 Happy are the servants whom their lord finds on the alert when he arrives. I assure you that he will then take off his outer clothes, make them sit down to dinner, and come and wait on them.

38 And if he should come just after midnight or in the very early morning, and find them still on the alert, their happiness is assured.

39 But be certain of this, that if the householder had known the time when the burglar would come, he would not have let his house be broken into.

40 So you must be on the alert, for the Son of Man is coming at a time when you may not expect him.'

41 Then Peter said to him,
'Lord, do you mean this parable for us or for everybody?'

42 But the Lord continued,
'Well, who will be the faithful, sensible steward whom his master will put in charge of his household to give them their supplies at the proper time?

43 Happy is the servant if his master finds him so doing when he returns.

44 I tell you he will promote him to look after all his property.

45 But suppose the servant says to himself, "My master takes his time about returning", and then begins to beat the men and women servants and to eat and drink and get drunk,

46 that servant's master will return suddenly and unexpectedly, and he will punish him severely and send him to share the penalty of the unfaithful.

47 The slave who knows his master's plan but does not get ready or act upon it will be severely punished,

48 but the servant who did not know the plan, though he has done wrong, will be let off lightly. Much will be expected from the one who has been given much, and the more a man is trusted, the more people will expect of him.'

The parable of the rich fool raised the question of man's latter end in its ordinary form – death. Christians have always seen their lives as directed to an end beyond that which is not something of their own contriving but, like the beginning, to be brought about by God. This means that one cannot know the 'how' or the 'when' of it, so must be ready for it at all times. The belief is taken over from Judaism's

expectation of the Day of the Lord but is focused in Christ
as God's deed and self-revelation. Men can know nothing
about the end except that he will be there. This is not an
incentive to do nothing but, on the contrary, to live well.
Although Luke is aware that much time has elapsed since
Jesus first proclaimed the end, it is still an essential part of
his thinking. The modern Christian is even more aware of
this vast postponement than Luke, yet he too sees the God
of Jesus as the standard, judge and goal of his existence and
so (perhaps metaphorically but certainly seriously) as that
end which is not in his control. He must leave it with God
and wait.

Verse 35 is a graphic picture of alertness, the long robe
caught up into the belt, the lamp burning. The last of these
is probably all that Luke retains of Matthew's parable of the
ten virgins which follows here (Matthew 25.1–13): verses 35–
38 are Luke's variation on Matthew's theme of watchfulness.
He has added a favourite motif, the common meal, as the
climax: with the surprising detail of the lord waiting on his
servants as in the feet-washing at supper in John 13.

Peter is brought forward at verse 41. As the leader of the
apostles he stands for all church-leaders. Luke's introduction
of him here resumes the theme of the interweaving of Jesus'
ministry and the church's and defines the scope of the parable
that follows. Here Luke follows Matthew very closely, for
their interests coincide on the theme of how to be a good
leader in the church, responsible to God for people. But
verses 47 and 48 are his own addition, similar in thought to
Amos 3. They soften the starkness of the previous picture
and will receive fuller and more graphic treatment at 19.11–
27, the parable of the talents.

12.49–53

49   'It is fire that I have come to bring upon the earth –
      how I could wish it were already ablaze!

50 There is a baptism that I must undergo and how strained
   I must be until it is all over!

51 'Do you think I have come to bring peace on the
   earth? No, I tell you, not peace, but division!

52 For from now on, there will be five people divided
   against each other in one house, three against two, and
   two against three.

53 It is going to be father against son, and son against
   father, mother against daughter, and daughter against
   mother; mother-in-law against daughter-in-law, and
   daughter-in-law against mother-in-law!'

The first two verses are peculiar to Luke, the second two
adapted from Matthew in a way which emphasizes the theme
of division. The whole is a passionate outburst which confronts the reader with the dark, troubled and aggressive
aspect which belongs to the gospel as to any creative act. It
also characterizes Jesus' ministry as a time of strain and
tension, a reminder that we are in the middle of a drama
not yet complete (Luke's sharp sense of time and development). *Fire* represents both the spirit and judgment. *Baptism*
refers to death (cf. Mark 10.38, Romans 6.3). Neither of these
points of resolution has yet been reached. The interim
before the end is therefore marked by unease and separation;
and it is *from now on*: an indication to the readers that as these
conditions prevailed beyond Golgotha and Pentecost into
the apostolic age of Acts, so they still go on. In a world that
is twisted and off-course, visitations of the creative spirit are
bound to be attended by conflict and hostility.

12.54–13.9

54 Then he said to the crowds,
   'When you see a cloud rising in the west, you say at
   once that it is going to rain, and so it does.

55 And when you feel the south wind blowing, you say that it is going to be hot, and so it is.

56 You frauds! You know how to interpret the look of the earth and the sky. Why can't you interpret the meaning of the times in which you live?

57   'And why can't you decide for yourselves what is right?

58 For instance, when you are going before the magistrate with your opponent, do your best to come to terms with him while you have the chance, or he may rush you off to the judge, and the judge hand you over to the police-officer, and the police-officer throw you into prison.

59 I tell you you will never get out again until you have paid your last farthing.'

1   It was just at this moment that some people came up to tell him the story of the Galileans whose blood Pilate had mixed with that of their sacrifices.

2 Jesus made this reply to them:
  'Are you thinking that these Galileans were worse sinners than any other men of Galilee because this happened to them?

3 I assure you that is not so. You will all die just as miserable a death unless your hearts are changed!

4 You remember those eighteen people who were killed at Siloam when the tower collapsed upon them? Are you imagining that they were worse offenders than any of the other people who lived in Jerusalem?

5 I assure you they were not. You will all die just as tragically unless your whole outlook is changed!'

6   Then he gave them this parable:
  'Once upon a time a man had a fig-tree growing in his vineyard, and when he came to look for the figs, he found none at all.

7   So he said to his gardener, "Look, I have come expecting
     fruit on this fig-tree for three years running and never
     found any. Better cut it down. Why should it use up
     valuable ground?"

8   And the gardener replied, "Master, don't touch it this
     year till I have had a chance to dig round it and give it a
     bit of manure.

9   Then, if it bears after that, it will be all right. But if it
     doesn't, then you can cut it down."'

The audience changes and the scope widens. From 12.22
it was the disciples. Now it is the crowds – everyone. The
disciples were told to be awake because their Lord could
return to his household at any time. Now everyone is told to
be awake to what is staring him in the face. Luke sees this
historically. He has in mind the imminent destruction of
Jerusalem by the Romans rather than some more theologi-
cal-symbolic end. The massacre of the Galileans and the
catastrophe at Siloam are pointers to it. But the moral is not
confined to the first century A.D. The words stand as an
injunction to watch political events seriously and discern
their direction; above all, to be ready to change one's mind
and act on what one sees. In this Jesus is the heir of the Old
Testament prophets.

Verses 54–56 are a recasting of Matthew 16.2–3. Whereas
Matthew's weather-lore is the rustic 'red sky at morning',
Luke goes by the wind. But why cannot, or dare not, people
be as perceptive about the human scene?

Verse 57 is Luke's and typical in its appeal to sense. Verses
58–59 are from Matthew's Sermon on the Mount, where the
emphasis of the context is on reconciliation and brotherhood.
But here it is an appeal to make a realistic assessment of a
situation and its possibilities and act accordingly. For Luke
this is a major theme and identical with repentance: see the
Prodigal Son of chapter 15 and the Steward of chapter 16.

Nothing is known outside this book of the two disasters in
13.1–5. The Galileans provided most of the members of the
Zealot (i.e. nationalist guerrilla) movement: Pilate was more
of a judicial thug than the gospels lead us to believe. It is a
likely incident, and so is the collapse of the tower. The words
just at this moment tie all this to the preceding section. Jesus'
informants seem to be ready for an interesting theological
discussion on the problem of evil, but he is brutal and direct.
This is what life is like, so they had better look to themselves
rather than speculate. Both incidents point menacingly to
the massacre and overthrow of A.D. 70 which Luke saw as
God's catastrophic judgment on his people.

Although the fig-tree parable is peculiar to Luke, Mark
11.12f. or Matthew 21.18f. is its source: an instance of how
easily an incident could become a parable or vice versa. The
fact that the tree stands in a vineyard[5] is incongruous to the
story, but to anyone who has read Isaiah 5 it is a broad hint
that Israel is under discussion. Although the nation is ripe
for destruction, now in Jesus' lifetime, it is allowed a short
period to change its ways.

13.10–21

10   It happened that he was teaching in one of the syna-
        gogues on the Sabbath day.
11   In the congregation was a woman who for eighteen
        years had been ill from some psychological cause; she
        was bent double and was quite unable to straighten
        herself up.
12   When Jesus noticed her, he called her and said,
            'You are set free from your illness!'
13   And he put his hands upon her, and at once she stood
        upright and praised God.

---

5. Phillips uses the word 'garden'.

14 But the president of the synagogue, in his annoyance at Jesus' healing on the Sabbath, announced to the congregation,

'There are six days in which men may work. Come on one of them and be healed, and not on the Sabbath day!'

15 But the Lord answered him, saying,

'You hypocrites, every single one of you unties his ox or his donkey from the stall and leads him away to water on the Sabbath day!

16 This woman, a daughter of Abraham, whom you all know Satan has kept bound for eighteen years – surely she should be released from such bonds on the Sabbath day!'

17 These words reduced his opponents to shame, but the crowd was thrilled at all the glorious things he did.

18 Then he went on,

'What is the kingdom of God like? What illustration can I use to make it plain to you?

19 It is like a grain of mustard-seed which a man took and dropped in his own garden. It grew and became a tree and the birds came and nested in its branches.'

20 Then he said again,

'What can I say the kingdom of God is like?

21 It is like the yeast which a woman took and covered up in three measures of flour until the whole had risen.'

It is hard to see what joins this to the preceding material unless it is the contrast between a twisted nation's inflexible refusal to change and the healing and straightening of one member of it: the woman's nationality is emphasized at verse 16. Luke's thinking, as often, moves from the many to the one and back again. Destruction and death are not the only possibilities for the Jews: Jesus brings restoration and life, though to the hard and fast legalists this is unacceptable because it does not come about in the approved way.

Though verse 15 is related to Matthew 12.11, this story is peculiar to Luke, and bears several of his trade-marks: the importance of women in his gospel, 'glorifying God' as a reaction to miracle, _daughter of Abraham_ (cf. 19.9 – Zacchaeus) which betrays his own kind of national-historical Jewish interest as against Matthew's 'law of Moses' interest, the pervading sense of the humanity of the gospel. The freeing of the woman from her illness and of the ox from its stall are connected by the use of the same Greek word for both. Jesus is the one who unties, sets free, liberates, so shaming his opponents and delighting everyone else.

The joining of Matthew's two little pictures of the mustard-seed and the yeast to this story might well have the following logic: as great things have small beginnings so this individual instance of liberation and healing could spread to restore the whole nation and more. Luke is indebted to Matthew for the pair of images and to Mark for the introduction (verse 18).

13.22–35

So he went on his way through towns and villages,
22 teaching as he went and making his way towards Jerusalem.

Someone asked him,

23 'Lord, are only a few men to be saved?'

And Jesus told them,

'You must try your hardest to get in through the
24 narrow door, for many, I assure you, will try to do so and will not succeed.

For once the master of the house has got up and shut
25 the door, you will find yourselves standing outside and knocking at the door crying, "Lord, please open the door for us." He will reply to you, "I don't know who you are or where you come from."

"But," you will protest, "we have had meals with you,
26 and you taught in our streets!"

27 Yet he will say to you, "I tell you I do not know where you have come from. Be off, you are all scoundrels!"

28 At that time there will be tears and bitter regret – to see Abraham and Isaac and Jacob and all the prophets inside the kingdom of God, and you yourselves banished outside!

29 Yes, and people will come from the east and the west, and from the north and the south, and take their seats in the kingdom of God.

30 There are some at the back now who will be in front then, and there are some in front now who will then be far behind.'

31 Just then some Pharisees arrived to tell him,
'You must get right away from here, for Herod intends to kill you.'

32 'Go and tell that fox,' returned Jesus, 'anyone can see that today and tomorrow I am expelling evil spirits and continuing my work of healing, and on the third day my work will be finished.

33 But I must journey on today, tomorrow, and the next day, for it would never do for a prophet to meet his death outside Jerusalem!

34 'O Jerusalem, Jerusalem, you murder the prophets and stone the messengers that are sent to you! How often have I longed to gather your children round me like a bird gathering her brood together under her wings, but you would never have it.

35 Now all you have left is your house. For I tell you that you will never see me again till the day when you cry, "Blessed is he who comes in the name of the Lord!"'

Matthew's favourite picture of Jesus is a rabbi in school instructing his disciples and arguing with his opponents: Luke's is a prophet in the world and in history. He modifies and amplifies his material accordingly. So this passage begins with a typically Lucan note of time and geography; re-arranges material from all over Matthew in verses 24–30; breaks into material of its own in verses 31–33 where the emphasis is on the story-line of Jesus' life; links this to the Matthean prophecy of the fall of Jerusalem in verses 34 and 35.

The sense of foreboding is established in verse 22 with its inexorable pointing towards Jerusalem. The teaching is woven into history from the start: particularly Jewish history and the fall of Jerusalem. Is this what is meant by the shutting of the door? Certainly the historical fact of the rejection of the Jews and inclusion of the Gentiles is being depicted here. Again Jesus meets a theoretical question with a practical answer: *You must try your hardest to get in through the narrow door*, i.e. the door into the kingdom of God. This reminds him of the excluded virgins in Matthew 25. It could be too late, and then no pleading will work, not even the (Lucan) one *we have had meals with you*: the theme of table-fellowship with Jesus which runs through this gospel, possibly also referring to the people of Israel in Exodus 24.11. Verses 29 and 30 are one of those little openings in this gospel through which we glimpse the future of Acts.

The friendly Pharisees of verse 31 may come as a surprise and are certainly a Lucan phenomenon. Gamaliel is a well-disposed Pharisee (Acts 5.34), and Acts 15.5 says that some Pharisees had joined the Christian church. Luke does not go all the way with Matthew in hostility to this sect. But the well-meant warning is disregarded. Jesus' destiny must unfold inevitably until it reaches the perfection of the resurrection on the third day (cf. 12.50, 18.31, 22.37 for other references to perfecting as the completion of the drama in the Easter events at Jerusalem). This typically Lucan note of dramatic time is followed by a lament over the city where all will be fulfilled. The *house* ('deserted' in some manuscripts) is the ruined Temple of A.D. 70, the coming of verse 35 the judgment of the Last Day – not all of which is contained in history for Luke.

The whole passage is typical of Luke's interest in the place of Jesus and his gospel in human life – here particularly in its political aspect and his call to take seriously both history and religion in the manner of the Old Testament historians.

14. 1–24

1   One Sabbath day he went into the house of one of the leading Pharisees for a meal, and they were watching him closely.

2   Right in front of him was a man afflicted with dropsy.

3   So Jesus spoke to the scribes and Pharisees and asked,
      'Well, is it right to heal on the Sabbath day or not?'

4   But there was no reply. So Jesus took the man and healed him and let him go.

5   Then he said to them,
      'If a donkey or an ox belonging to one of you fell into a well, wouldn't you rescue it without the slightest hesitation even though it were the Sabbath?'

6   And this again left them quite unable to reply.

7   Then he gave a pointed word of advice to the guests when he noticed how they were choosing the best seats. He said to them,

8   'When you are invited to a wedding reception, don't sit down in the best seat. It might happen that a more distinguished man than you has also been invited.

9   Then your host might say, "I am afraid you must give up your seat for this man." And then, with considerable embarrassment, you will have to sit in the humblest place.

10   No, when you are invited, go and take your seat in an inconspicuous place, so that when your host comes in he may say to you, "Come on, my dear fellow, we have

a much better seat than this for you." That is the way to be important in the eyes of all your fellow-guests!

11 For everyone who makes himself important will become insignificant, while the man who makes himself insignificant will find himself important.'

12 Then, addressing his host, Jesus said,

'When you give a luncheon or dinner-party, don't invite your friends or your brothers or relations or wealthy neighbours, for the chances are they will invite you back, and you will be fully repaid.

13 No, when you give a party, invite the poor, the crippled, the lame and the blind.

14 That way lies real happiness for you. They have no means of repaying you, but you will be repaid when good men are rewarded – at the resurrection.'

15 Then, one of the guests, hearing these remarks of Jesus, said,

'What happiness for a man to eat a meal in the kingdom of God!'

16 But Jesus said to him,

'Once upon a time, a man planned a big dinner-party and invited a great many people.

17 At dinner-time, he sent his servant out to tell those who were invited, "Please come, everything is now ready."

18 But they all, as one man, began to make their excuses. The first one said to him, "I have bought some land. I must go and look at it. Please excuse me."

19 Another one said, "I have bought five yoke of oxen and am on my way to try them out. Please convey my apologies."

20 And another one said, "I have just got married and I am sure you will understand I cannot come."

21 So the servant returned and reported all this to his master. The master of the house was extremely annoyed and said to his servant, "Hurry out now into the streets

and alleys of the town, and bring here the poor and crippled and blind and lame."

22 Then the servant said, "I have done what you told me, sir, and there are still empty places."

23 Then the master replied, "Now go out to the roads and hedgerows and make them come inside, so that my house may be full.

24 For I tell you that not one of the men I invited shall have a taste of my dinner." '

We switch from the grand scene to the domestic. The table is a favourite setting of Luke's (cf. 7.36, 11.37, 24.30). There was precedent for this in secular literature like Plato's symposium and in the Epistle of Aristeas, a work of Jewish apologetic. Luke's middle-class affinities come out in the comparative affluence of the people in the parables who belong to a class where entertaining is part of life. Here, then, is Jesus' table-talk.

The dropsical man is peculiar to Luke, but the argument about doing good on the Sabbath is common to all the synoptics, and verse 5 is in Matthew 12.11. The decisive point is that in practice love and need override law – not love in any grand emotional sense so much as in care for anything of one's own that is threatened. His opponents' inability to reply is an unwilling assent to the gospel which (for Luke particularly) is about the rescue of the lost.

The witty advice to guests and hosts is in Luke alone. The crux of the first is: 'Don't put yourself in a position where you could be made to look silly.' Not a very exalted appeal, but because Luke calls it a parable it is a figurative utterance which applies to the kingdom of God where the mighty are put down from their seats and the humble are set in honour (verse 11, cf. 1.52 and Proverbs 25.6). This kind of worldly wisdom was popular with the Jews and welcome to Luke with his more world-affirming outlook. The high-minded

neglect it at their peril. The argument of the advice to hosts
is: 'Be more adventurous, break out of the narrow circle
where kindness is immediately and safely returned and risk
more to get more.' It is a nice counterpoise to the prudential
advice to guests, and further witness to the reversal which is
central to the gospel. The resurrection of the just was a
Jewish belief before it became a Christian one (Acts 26.6–8).

The parable of the *big dinner-party* is a trimmed-up version of
Matthew 22.1–14. Matthew slanted it towards the Jewish
nation and the destruction of Jerusalem. Luke has already
dealt with this so uses it in a psychological way as an illustration of the reasons people give for not attending the
banquet of God's kingdom. The introductory verse 15
(peculiar to Luke) makes it clear that it is all about the feast
of the kingdom. Matthew's king with many servants becomes
a man with one. For Matthew big parties were unfamiliar:
the sort of thing royalty do. For Luke they are part of life.
He also drops the symbolism of its being a marriage feast.
Then he gives each guest a little speech, omits Matthew's
exaggerated account of the destruction of the city together
with the expulsion of the improperly dressed diner, and
reaches a resounding conclusion. Luke's version is certainly
more unified and satisfying than Matthew's, and so is the
one which people usually remember.

In verses 21–24 there is an allegory which points towards
the future of Acts. First the poor of the city (namely
Jerusalem) are called – the under-privileged Jews. Then the
invitation reaches into the *roads and hedgerows* of the outer
world – the Gentiles. Finally the doom of the first-invited
guests is sealed – the rejection of the Jews. We are given a
sketch for Acts in a picture of good news coming as an
invitation to a party. The rejection of it by those too pre-
occupied to be bothered only serves to force it out into a
wider area. There is no stopping it.

25   Now as Jesus proceeded on his journey, great crowds accompanied him, and he turned and spoke to them,

26   'If anyone comes to me without "hating" his father and mother and wife and children and brothers and sisters, and even his own life, he cannot be a disciple of

27   mine. The man who will not take up his cross and follow in my footsteps cannot be my disciple.

28   'If any of you wanted to build a tower, wouldn't he first sit down and work out the cost of it, to see if he can afford to finish it?

29   Otherwise, when he has laid the foundation and found himself unable to complete the building, everyone who sees it will begin to jeer at him,

30   saying, "This is the man who started to build a tower but couldn't finish it!"

31   Or, suppose there is a king who is going to war with another king, doesn't he sit down first and consider whether he can engage the twenty thousand of the other king with his own ten thousand?

32   And if he decides he can't, then, while the other king is still a long way off, he sends messengers to him to ask for conditions of peace.

33   So it is with you; only the man who says goodbye to all his possessions can be my disciple.

34   'Salt is a very good thing, but if salt loses its flavour, what can you use to restore it?

35   It is no good for the ground and no good as manure. People just throw it away. Every man who has ears should use them!'

The section opens with a reminder of the journey and a switch-back to the public setting of *great crowds*. As in the previous chapter (13.24), the parables are followed by a sharp and demanding saying. This in turn is illustrated.

Verse 26 is not an invitation to resentment, but a strong and exaggerated way of saying that discipleship must take the priority over everything. Discipleship consists of two things: taking up one's own cross (bearing and not evading one's destiny and difficulties) and following Jesus on his way to God. Any sensible person would think twice before deciding to meet such a demand, so Luke follows it with some of that worldly wisdom and good sense which we have found to be characteristic of him. Verses 28–33 are nothing if not pragmatic and typically Lucan in their middle-class and ruling class setting. Response to Jesus' call is represented in terms of financial and military adventure which, grandly exciting as they are, require a cool head and a sound business sense. It does not detract from the gospel summons to present it in this prudential fashion; rather it adds a welcome touch of realism. Luke is against sentimental enthusiasm (11.27, 14.15, 23.27) and represents Jesus as bringing it down to earth. But verse 33 shows that he in no way edits the sharpness of the issue.

The salt saying is from Mark and Matthew, adapted by Luke to point his argument that only the real thing is worthwhile.

15

1　Now all the tax-collectors and 'outsiders' were crowding around to hear what he had to say.

2　The Pharisees and the scribes complained of this, remarking,

'This man welcomes sinners and even eats his meals with them.'

3　So Jesus spoke to them, using this parable:

4　'Wouldn't any man among you who owned a hundred sheep, and lost one of them, leave the ninety-nine to themselves in the open, and go after the one which is lost until he finds it?

5 And when he has found it, he will lift it on to his shoulders with great joy,

6 and as soon as he gets home, he will call his friends and neighbours together. "Rejoice with me," he will say, "for I have found that sheep of mine which was lost."

7 I tell you that it is the same in Heaven – there is more joy over one sinner whose heart is changed than over ninety-nine righteous people who have no need for repentance.

8 'Or if a woman who has ten silver coins should lose one, won't she take a lamp and sweep and search the house from top to bottom until she finds it?

9 And when she has found it, she calls her friends and neighbours together. "Rejoice with me," she says, "for I have found that coin I lost."

10 I tell you, it is the same in Heaven – there is rejoicing among the angels of God over one sinner whose heart is changed.'

11 Then he continued,

'Once there was a man who had two sons.

12 The younger one said to his father, "Father, give me my share of the property that will come to me." So he divided up his estate between the two of them.

13 Before very long, the younger son collected all his belongings and went off to a distant land, where he squandered his wealth in the wildest extravagance.

14 And when he had run through all his money, a terrible famine arose in that country, and he began to feel the pinch.

15 Then he went and hired himself out to one of the citizens of that country who sent him out into the fields to feed the pigs.

16 He got to the point of longing to stuff himself with the husks the pigs were eating, and not a soul gave him anything.

17 Then he came to his senses and cried aloud, "Why, dozens of my father's hired men have more food than they can eat and here am I dying of hunger!

18 I will get up and go back to my father, and I will say to him, 'Father, I have done wrong in the sight of Heaven and in your eyes.

19 I don't deserve to be called your son any more. Please take me on as one of your hired men.' "

20 So he got up and went to his father. But while he was still some distance off, his father saw him and his heart went out to him, and he ran and fell on his neck and kissed him.

21 But his son said, "Father, I have done wrong in the sight of Heaven and in your eyes. I don't deserve to be called your son any more . . ."

22 "Hurry!" called out his father to the servants, "fetch the best clothes and put them on him! Put a ring on his finger and shoes on his feet,

23 and get that fatted calf and kill it, and we will have a feast and a celebration!

24 For this is my son – he was dead, and he's alive again. He was lost, and now he's found!" And they began to get the festivities going.

25 'But his elder son was out in the fields, and as he came near the house, he heard music and dancing.

26 So he called one of the servants across to him and enquired what was the meaning of it all.

27 "Your brother has arrived, and your father has killed the fatted calf because he has got him home again safe and sound," was the reply.

28 But he was furious and refused to go inside the house. So his father came outside and pleaded with him.

29 Then he burst out, "Look, how many years have I slaved for you and never disobeyed a single order of yours, and yet you have never given me so much as a

young goat so that I could give my friends a dinner?
30 But when this son of yours arrives, who has spent all your money on prostitutes, for him you kill the fatted calf!"
31 But the father replied, "My dear son, you have been with me all the time and everything I have is yours.
33 But we had to celebrate and show our joy. For this is your brother; he was dead – and he's alive. He was lost – and now he is found!" '

'Better to have loved and lost, than never to have loved at all' – and better still to have loved and lost and found again, which is the reason for the rejoicing in these parables. God's love for sinners and outsiders is a major theme of Luke's. So is joy. Here the two come together, joined by another of Luke's themes: repentance, meaning a change or turning of mind and heart. This is tacked on to the two little pictures, but it is bound into the story of the Prodigal Son and so made more explicit.

Verse 1 sets the scene. It is triangular: Jesus, sinners, Pharisees. In the light of the gospel the opposite of goodness is not the sinner but the self-righteous and resentful 'good man' – a suggestion to which few can adapt themselves.

The lost sheep comes from Matthew 18.12–13. There it is about the erring Christian brother, but here it has an un-ecclesiastical and wider setting. Luke has laid on more rejoicing in verse 6: the shepherd cannot contain his happiness and makes it social. He also emphasizes the change of heart in a sinner which gives rise to similar social hilarity in the court of Heaven.

The lost coin parable is Luke's own. There is no need to posit any other source than the previous illustration which provides the pattern. Clearly Matthew's lost sheep interested and excited Luke enough for him to want to repeat its message and structure here and, more elaborately, in the subsequent story. The woman in the house is as typical of him as the money interest, and balances the man in the countryside. Again, her happiness is an image of the joy in God's household when a sinner changes course.

The trouble with these two pictures is that they do not really dramatize Luke's main point – repentance. The sheep does not undergo a change of heart, still less the coin. For that he needs a human being instead of an animal or thing. So there follows the story of the lost son in which the theme of lost-and-found, which Matthew's lost sheep had sparked off in Luke's mind, finds its most unforgettable expression. Like the other long story of the Good Samaritan it bears many of Luke's trade-marks: a secular story without religious trappings, the well-to-do setting (people of property, with servants), journeying, the moment when dereliction turns to comfort, reference to the moral outer-fringes and the Old Testament.

There is a certain allegorical aspect to the story. The father's gifts in verse 22 have their meanings: a robe was honorific (in Heaven God's people would be given new robes – Revelation 6.11), the ring signified authority, and shoes were for freemen. Further than that, verses 1 and 2 suggest that there may well be something in the old interpretation which sees the father as God, the elder son as orthodox pharisaical Judaism, the younger son as the un-respectable kind of Jew who became a Christian (N.B. he is *not* a Gentile).

But the main interest of the story will always be its insight into the workings of the human heart and portrayal of contrasted characters. The father is the original good parent who, for all his fondness for him, lets his child go without question and, for all the distress he has caused, receives him back without recrimination. The younger son is a figure of youth with its ambiguous thirst for experience. His grief at the failure of his schemes does not deprive him of the mental resilience to see sense (very Lucan) and get out of it. The elder son is middle-aged in mentality if not years, a righteous and dutiful type who resents the fact that neither his father nor the way of the world is as morally tidy as he has made his own existence. His character is reminiscent of Jonah. The two brothers are thus played off against one another, but it is not a plain contrast of virtue and nastiness. Each misbehaves in his characteristic fashion. The goodness is with the uncondemning and deeply generous father. If the younger son is in a better position to appreciate that, it is only because he has made a worse mess of his life. We are not told whether the elder brother joined the party and enjoyed it but must hope that he did because that would be his act of repentance. Luke prefers to finish the tale with the triumphant joy which he can best express in the Christian terms of resurrection from the dead. (Cf. Genesis 46.29–30.)

16. 1–15

1   Then there is this story he told his disciples:
     'Once there was a rich man whose agent was reported to him to be mismanaging his property.
2   So he summoned him and said, "What's this that I hear about you? Give me an account of your stewardship – you're not fit to manage my household any longer."
3   At this the agent said to himself, "What am I going to do now that my employer is taking away the management from me? I am not strong enough to dig and I can't sink to begging.
4   Ah, I know what I'll do so that when I lose my position people will welcome me into their homes!"
5   So he sent for each one of his master's debtors. "How much do you owe my master?" he said to the first.
6   "A hundred barrels of oil," he replied. "Here," replied the agent, "take your bill, sit down, hurry up and write in fifty."

7   Then he said to another, "And what's the size of your debt?" "A thousand bushels of wheat," he replied. "Take your bill," said the agent, "and write in eight hundred."

8   Now the master praised this rascally agent because he had been so careful for his own future. For the children of this world are considerably more shrewd in dealing with their contemporaries than the children of light.

9   Now my advice to you is to use "money", tainted as it is, to make yourselves friends, so that when it comes to an end, they may welcome you into the houses of eternity.

10   'The man who is faithful in the little things will be faithful in the big things, and the man who cheats in the little things will cheat in the big things too.

11   So that if you are not fit to be trusted to deal with the wicked wealth of this world, who will trust you with the true riches?

12   And if you are not trustworthy with someone else's property, who will give you property of your own?

13   No servant can serve two masters. He is bound to hate one and love the other, or give his loyalty to one and despise the other. You cannot serve God and the power of money at the same time.'

14   Now the Pharisees, who were very fond of money, heard all this with a sneer.

15   But he said to them,
     'You are the people who advertise your goodness before men, but God knows your hearts. Remember, there are things men consider splendid which are detestable in the sight of God!'

Those who sympathized with the elder rather than the younger brother will hardly enjoy this story. Here Luke takes his fondness for worldly wisdom to quite outrageous lengths: the steward certainly has no other quality for which

the master could praise him. Luke has a way of using un-
edifying characters as examples of right response to a crisis
(cf. the reluctant friend, 11.8 and the unjust judge, 18.2).
The reader is teased to pursue his salvation as ruthlessly as
others go after making money or salvaging their own
interests and reputations. There are more of his trade-marks
in the passage: a wealthy environment again and a soliloquy
which lets us in on the man's thinking (as with the prodigal
son). The day of audit is a secular, everyday image of God's
judgment. Both in the story and more evidently in the
collection of maxims which follows it he is addressing the
moneyed class and exhorting them to use their wealth
shrewdly in the service of God. The amorality of the parable
has long given offence to nice-minded church people and
critics, some of whom have suggested that the string of
proverbs which follows it shows that it embarrassed Luke too,
though somehow he felt that he must include it. Against
this it may be said that the whole thing is very much Luke. He
is letting rip on a favourite theme. If he challenges the
lingering pharisaism of his readers, so much the better. In
any case, verse 13, which quotes Matthew 6.24, brings it all
home safely enough: the service of God is the overriding
factor. And verses 14 and 15 are a sharp enough answer to
those who judge by external standards of moral hygiene:
honi soit qui mal y pense!

16.16–18

16 'The Law and the Prophets were in force until John's
day. From then on the good news of the kingdom of
God has been proclaimed and everyone is trying to force
his way into it.

17 'Yet it would be easier for Heaven and earth to disappear than for a single point of the Law to become a
dead letter.

18　'Any man who divorces his wife and marries another
　　woman commits adultery. And so does any man who
　　marries the woman who was divorced from her hus-
　　band.'

This passage is something of a job-lot. Verse 16 connects
well enough with the crafty steward: in the old days all was
settled, but now that the gospel-time has begun the situation
is critical and a matter of *sauve qui peut*. Such seems to be the
sense of Luke's adaptation of Matthew 11.12–13. But verse 17
modifies it: the law still stands. Matthew (5.18) is again the
source. Possibly the conjunction of the two verses bears
witness to the perennial Christian ambiguity about moral
rules: they are indispensable but they are not salvation.
The ruling on divorce is tougher than in Matthew 5.32,
more Jewish (i.e. only the man can do it) than at Mark
10.11–12, so there was some variation about this in the early
church.

16.19–31

19　'There was once a rich man who used to dress in
　　purple and fine linen and lead a life of daily luxury.
20　And there was a poor man called Lazarus who was put
　　down at his gate. He was covered with sores.
21　He used to long to be fed with the scraps from the rich
　　man's table. Yes, and the dogs used to come and lick
　　his sores.
22　Well, it happened that the poor man died, and was
　　carried by the angels into Abraham's bosom. The rich
　　man also died and was buried.
23　And from the place of the dead he looked up in torment
　　and saw Abraham a long way away, and Lazarus in his
　　arms.
24　"Father Abraham!" he cried out, "please pity me! Send

Lazarus to dip the tip of his finger in water and cool my tongue, for I am in agony in these flames."

25 But Abraham replied, "Remember, my son, that you used to have the good things in your lifetime, just as Lazarus suffered the bad. Now he is being comforted here, while you are in agony.

26 And besides this, a great chasm has been set between you and us, so that those who want to go to you from this side cannot do so, and people cannot come to us from your side."

27 At this he said, "Then I beg you, father, to send him to my father's house

28 for I have five brothers. He could warn them and prevent their coming to this place of torture."

29 But Abraham said, "They have Moses and the Prophets: they can listen to them."

30 "Ah no, father Abraham," he said, "if only someone were to go to them from the dead, they would change completely."

31 But Abraham told him, "If they will not listen to Moses and the Prophets, they would not be convinced even if somebody were to rise from the dead." '

We return to the matter of money. The story has two halves, the division falling between verses 26 and 27. The first half is very likely Luke's version of a widespread folk tale about the reversal of fortunes in the after-life which would certainly appeal to the writer of the Magnificat. An Egyptian papyrus of the first century tells a similar tale, ending: 'It was ordered by Osiris that the grave clothes of the rich man [which were magnificent] should be given to the poor man, and that the poor man should be placed among the splendidly transfigured ones.' Whereas the crafty agent was exemplary, the rich man is a horrible warning. Luke is bringing home the importance of Christian aid to his well-

to-do readers. We notice his Jewishness in the central place
which Abraham occupies in paradise: a contrast with the
similar Matthew 25.31–46 where it is Jesus as Son of Man.
Luke is particularly fond of Abraham (1.55 and 73, 13.16,
19.9) as the historic father of God's people.

From verse 27 the story is about resurrection. Even the
rich man has his points: he does not want his five brothers
to share his fate *If only someone were to go to them from the dead,
they would change completely*. But Abraham knows better, and the
words which Luke gives him are no doubt informed by bitter
experience of the failure of the Jews to change on account of
Christ's resurrection. Those who do not attend to the smaller
things of God, such as the care for one's neighbour which
Law and prophets enjoined, are not open to his great works.

17.1–10

1 Then Jesus said to his disciples,
    'It is inevitable that there should be pitfalls, but alas
    for the man who is responsible for them!
2 It would be better for that man to have a mill-stone
    hung round his neck and be thrown into the sea, than
    that he should trip up one of these little ones.
3 So be careful how you live. If your brother offends you,
    take him to task about it, and if he is sorry, forgive him.
4 Yes, if he wrongs you seven times in one day and turns
    to you and says, "I am sorry" seven times, you must
    forgive him.'
5 And the apostles said to the Lord,
    'Give us more faith.'
6 And he replied,
    'If your faith were as big as a grain of mustard-seed,
    you could say to this mulberry tree, "Pull yourself up
    by the roots and plant yourself in the sea," and it would
    obey you!

7 'If any of you has a servant ploughing or looking after the sheep, are you likely to say to him when he comes in from the fields, "Come straight in and sit down to your meal"?

8 Aren't you more likely to say, "Get my supper ready: change your coat, and wait on me while I eat and drink: and then, when I've finished, you can have your meal"?

9 Do you feel grateful to your servant for doing what you tell him? I don't think so.

10 It is the same with yourselves – when you have done everything that you are told to do, you can say, "We are not much good as servants; we have only done what we ought to do." '

Three sayings about pitfalls, forgiveness and faith taken from Matthew 17 and 18 are followed by Luke's own illustration of reasonable service. His habit of splitting up teaching material which Matthew has organized in blocks with a single theme makes for rather disjointed reading. That is the price he has to pay for holding his reader's attention by interspersing the preaching with stories and narrative. The commentator has to discover connections which are far from obvious.

The saying about pitfalls must be a reflection on the careless rich man. The fact of evil is taken for granted (cf. the tower at Siloam), but this does not exculpate those who propagate it and hurt others. The only remedy is forgiveness and in this the disciple must set no limit. The saying about faith is addressed by *the Lord* (Christian title for Jesus) to *the apostles* (leaders of the Christian church). The apostles' request comes, perhaps, from their awareness of the difficulty of the life outlined in the previous sayings. The reply is, of course, hyperbolic and not to be taken literally. Faith is that combination of persistence and expectation which is distinct from giving up on the one hand and force on the other.

There is no apparent connection between this and the servant illustration which follows and is peculiar to Luke. It is typical of him with its setting in a well-to-do household and its appeal to worldly common sense. Its message is that no one can do God a favour. Whatever is done for him is no more than our bounden duty and not matter for self-congratulation.

17. 11–19

11 In the course of his journey to Jerusalem, Jesus crossed the boundary between Samaria and Galilee,

12 and as he was approaching a village, ten lepers met him. They kept their distance

13 but shouted out,
    'Jesus, Master, have pity on us!'

14 When Jesus saw them, he said,
    'Go and show yourselves to the priests.'
    And it happened that as they went on their way they were cured.

15 One of their number, when he saw that he was healed, turned round and praised God at the top of his voice,

16 and then fell on his face before Jesus and thanked him. This man was a Samaritan.

17 And at this Jesus remarked,
    'Weren't there ten men cured? Where are the other nine?

18 Is nobody going to turn and praise God, except this stranger?'

19 And he said to the man,
    'Stand up now, and go on your way. It is your faith that has made you well.'

Though related to Mark 1.40–44 (possibly its source) this story is peculiar to Luke and has his characteristic marks: a reminder of the journey to Jerusalem, the goodness of a Samaritan, praising God as the response to a miracle. There does not seem to be any particular reason why this incident should have been put just here in the book unless the Samaritan is seen as the one who does his duty in returning to give thanks; or Luke is taking up the theme of the strength of faith from verse 6. Perhaps both. But the main point is in verse 16. Jesus gets a better response from suspected people like the Samaritans than he does from more orthodox Jewry. But again (cf. 9.52ff.) no Samaritan town is entered. That will happen in Acts.

17.20–37

20   Later, he was asked by the Pharisees when the kingdom of God was coming, and he gave them this reply:
'The kingdom of God never comes by looking for signs of it.

21   Men cannot say, "Look, here it is", or "there it is", for the kingdom of God is inside you.'

22   Then he said to the disciples,
'The time will come when you will long to see again a single day of the Son of Man, but you will not see it.

23   People will say to you, "Look, there it is", or "Look, here it is." Stay where you are and don't follow them!

24   For the day of the Son of Man will be like lightning flashing from one end of the sky to the other.

25   But before that happens, he must go through much suffering and be utterly rejected by this generation.

26   In the time of the coming of the Son of Man, life will be as it was in the days of Noah.

27   People ate and drank, married and were given in marriage, right up to the day when Noah entered the ark –

and then came the flood and destroyed them all.

28 It will be just the same as it was in the days of Lot. People ate and drank, bought and sold, planted and built,

29 but on the day that Lot left Sodom, it rained fire and brimstone from Heaven, and destroyed them all.

30 That is how it will be on the day when the Son of Man is revealed.

31 When that day comes, the man who is on the roof of his house, with his goods inside it, must not come down to get them. And the man out in the fields must not turn back for anything.

32 Remember what happened to Lot's wife.

33 Whoever tries to keep his life safe will lose it, and the man who is prepared to lose his life will preserve it.

34 I tell you, that night there will be two men in one bed; one man will be taken and the other will be left.

35 Two women will be turning the grinding-mill together; one will be taken and the other left.'

37 'But when, Lord?' they asked him.

'Wherever there is a dead body, there the vultures will flock,' he replied.

The passage is made up of extracts from Matthew 24, but not in the same order, interspersed with Luke's own contributions. The style is apocalyptic as distinct from the more historical doom in chapter 21. It is a disclosure in some detail of things yet to come like the book of Daniel or John's Apocalypse. This is a very hot and dangerous literary form which, for all its resounding splendour, can verge on the lunatic. Luke is not against it, or he would not have put it in, but he does impose controls of his own: verses 20 and 21 point to the present rather than a visionary future, verse 25 brings it down to the history of Jesus' own life, verses 28 and 29 emphasize its sudden incalculability. All these verses are peculiar to Luke, and so is the riddle of verse 37. The general message is that the last day will be sudden even if it has been delayed.

Verse 20 shows that Luke is aware that apocalyptic speculation was an interest of the Pharisees whose belief in the 'last things' was condemned by the conservative Sadducees: so the question comes from them. Jesus' answer is not paralleled in the other gospels but only in the late Oxyrhynchus Papyrus and the gospel of Thomas: 'The kingdom is within you and outside you.' Phillips' *inside* could also be 'among', but that does not alter the uniqueness of this assertion of the kingdom settled within human life rather than breaking into it from outside. The saying is unforgettable and testifies to the greater value which Luke sets on present worldly life than the other gospel-writers.

It contrasts strongly with the futurist material which follows. The church's longing for the great resolution is reflected in verse 22. But there is no need to look for it. When it happens it will be clear enough, though first Jesus' life and rejection must run their course and be completed. Noah's flood and the destruction of Sodom emphasize its catastrophic suddenness. Verse 31 is puzzling. There will, presumably, be no escaping the last judgment. But the advice would make good sense in the events leading up to A.D. 70 – run from the Roman army! Verse 37 chimes in with this – *vultures* circling over the massacre at Jerusalem. Verses 34 and 36 are about the swift, almost arbitrary, separation which the judgment will bring about.

So we have here apocalyptic, earthed and modified by its references to the kingdom in our midst, to the course of the life and death of Jesus and to the destruction of Jerusalem. Speculation about the latter days is unnecessary because all that matters about them is already impinging and staring Jesus' listeners in the face.

18. 1–17

1   Then he gave them an illustration to show that they
     must always pray and never lose heart.

2   'Once upon a time,' he said, 'there was a magistrate in
     a town who had neither fear of God nor respect for his
     fellow-men.

3   There was a widow in the town who kept coming to
     him, saying, "Please protect me from the man who is
     trying to ruin me."

4   And for a long time he refused. But later he said to
     himself, "Although I don't fear God and have no respect
     for men,

5   yet this woman is such a nuisance that I shall give
     judgment in her favour, or else her continual visits
     will be the death of me!"'

6   Then the Lord said,

7   'Notice how this dishonest magistrate behaved. Do
     you suppose God, patient as he is, will not see justice
     done for his chosen, who appeal to him day and night?

8   I assure you he will not delay in seeing justice done. Yet,
     when the Son of Man comes, will he find men on earth
     who believe in him?'

9   Then he gave this illustration to certain people who
     were confident of their own goodness and looked down
     on others:

10   'Two men went up to the Temple to pray, one was a
     Pharisee, the other was a tax-collector.

11   The Pharisee stood and prayed like this with himself,
     "O God, I do thank thee that I am not like the rest of
     mankind, greedy, dishonest, impure, or even like that
     tax-collector over there.

12   I fast twice every week; I give away a tenth-part of all my
     income."

13   But the tax-collector stood in a distant corner, scarcely

daring to look up to Heaven, and with a gesture of despair, said, "God have mercy on a sinner like me."

14 I assure you that he was the man who went home justified in God's sight, rather than the other one. For everyone who sets himself up as somebody will become a nobody, and the man who makes himself nobody will become somebody.'

15 Then people began to bring babies to him that he could put his hands on them. But when the disciples noticed it, they frowned on them.

16 But Jesus called them to him, and said,

'You must let little children come to me, and you must never prevent their coming. The kingdom of God belongs to little children like these.

17 I tell you, the man who will not accept the kingdom of God like a little child will never get into it at all.'

The section consists of two parables peculiar to Luke, followed by an incident from Mark. All of them show the divine acceptance of defenceless and indefensible people. The two parables are linked by another favourite theme of Luke's – prayer. Notice that they are not specifically Christian. They concern man's standing before God, a matter as central to Judaism as to Christianity.

A widow in the ancient world was very insecure, lost in a masculine society with no man to defend her. The only tactic was to make a weapon of defencelessness. There is nothing to do but cry, so she cries away as hard as she can and weakness becomes a strange strength. In this she displays that shrewdness which Luke admires. In a typically Lucan soliloquy the judge also opts for the common-sensical course and she gets her rights. The introduction makes it clear that for Luke prayer means asking and beseeching. 'Wants are the ligatures that tie us to God, whereby we live in him and feel his enjoyments.' (Thomas Traherne) The explanation at the end with its how-much-more appeal points to a God who is accessible to the crying of his people and will do things for them. Verse 8b is disconnected and perhaps looks back to the previous section. Petitionary prayer is strong in the sense that, like the widow, we continually and uninhibitedly present ourselves and our cause to God; weak in that we leave the answer to him. It is not resignation and it is not blackmail.

The next parable contrasts prayer as the expression of smug contentment and prayer as beseeching. The Pharisee prays from a position of strength: he cannot, for example, 'be said to be tempted to steal, for, should the idea of stealing occur to him, he will immediately dismiss it from his mind as something that is "not done"; every time the idea of stealing occurs to the Publican it requires a moral effort to resist for which he may not have the strength.' (W. H. Auden) The tax-collector, by definition a swindler, prays from a position of weakness. He is justified because his is a real prayer, while the Pharisee's is, strictly speaking, not a prayer at all. If God is the God of the Magnificat, verse 14 is the obvious conclusion. Again, the glimpse into people's inmost thoughts which forms the crux of the parable is typical of Luke.

At verse 15 Luke picks up Mark's gospel again. At 9.50 he had dropped it in favour of Matthew (or 'Q') with his wealth of teaching. The resumption is a sign that we are going to have less instruction and more narrative. But this change of source makes no break in the flow of Luke's work. The incident of the babies connects well with the helpless people in the two parables preceding. The kingdom of God is for those whose need makes them open to receive it in simplicity.

18. 18–30

18 Then one of the Jewish rulers put this question to him,

'Master, I know that you are good; tell me, please, what must I do to be sure of eternal life?'

19 'I wonder why you call me good?' returned Jesus. 'No one is good – only the one God.

20 You know the commandments –

'Thou shalt not commit adultery.

'Thou shalt not commit murder.

'Thou shalt not steal.

'Thou shalt not bear false witness.

'Honour thy father and thy mother.'

21 'All these,' he replied, 'I have carefully kept since I was quite young.'

22 And when Jesus heard that, he said to him,

'There is still one thing you have missed. Sell everything you possess and give the money away to the poor, and you will have riches in Heaven. Then come and follow me.'

23 But when he heard this, he was greatly distressed for he was very rich.

24 And when Jesus saw how his face fell, he remarked,

'How difficult it is for those who have great possessions to enter the kingdom of God!

25 A camel could squeeze through the eye of a needle more easily than a rich man could get into the kingdom of God.'

26 Those who heard Jesus say this, exclaimed,

'Then who can possibly be saved?'

27 Jesus replied,

'What men find impossible is possible with God.'

28 'Well,' rejoined Peter, 'we have left all that we ever had and followed you.'

29   And Jesus told them,
      'Believe me, nobody has left his home or wife, or
      brothers or parents or children for the sake of the
      kingdom of God,
30   without receiving very much more in this present life –
      and eternal life in the world to come.'

Luke has lopped off some of the details of Mark's story
(Mark 10.17–31) so as to let the theme of renunciation of
possessions stand out more clearly. Mark's man becomes a
ruler, with typical Lucan emphasis. He asks the crucial and
radical question which has been asked before at 10.25. Here
the answer is direct moral theology and not a secular story.
Jesus rebukes his flattery and returns a traditional answer.
Has the ruler taken seriously what he already knows of the
will of God? Assured that he has, Jesus makes a further
radical demand, renunciation of all his wealth – but notice
that there is promise and the life of discipleship as well as
renunciation: Jesus is not asking for a vacuum. The ruler's
obvious disappointment gives rise to an exclamation from
Jesus and a brisk exchange with the people around and Peter,
as representative disciple. The camel and the needle's eye is
strong speech to dramatize impossibility, but the humanly
impossible is possible with God. Peter, on behalf of the rest
of the disciples, claims that they have fulfilled the call to
renounce. Jesus puts that in the shade by pointing to the
incalculable reward which is theirs *in this present life – and . . . in
the world to come.*

7

Near Jerusalem

18.31–34

31 Then Jesus took the Twelve on one side and spoke to
   them,
      'Listen to me. We are now going up to Jerusalem and
   everything that has been written by the prophets about
   the Son of Man will come true.

32 For he will be handed over to the heathen, and he is
   going to be jeered at and insulted and spat upon,

33 and then they will flog him and kill him. But he will rise
   again on the third day.'

34   But they did not understand any of this. His words
   were quite obscure to them and they had no idea of
   what he meant.

As we emerge from the long teaching section the narrative
thrust of the gospel comes out more clearly with its note of
doom and triumph. Luke has tried to keep us aware of it by
his frequent notes about being on the road to Jerusalem.
But this was only partially successful, and the sense of
movement only very slight. That has changed now, for he
has laid aside Matthew (his main source for teaching) and
picked up Mark (his main source for narrative). There will
be teaching certainly and he will have to resort to Matthew
again, but it will be supported by a more urgent situation
which points towards Easter. This little section is like a bell
summoning the reader back to the drama.

Luke has adapted Mark's version (Mark 10.32–34), leaving
out the note of fear and dread at the beginning, adding,

characteristically, the note about the fulfilment of the prophetic writings (cf. 22.37, 24.25, 44), *insult* to the sufferings of verse 32, and the whole of verse 34. This latter, the incomprehension of the disciples, is a major theme of Mark's which Luke handles more sparingly. The twelve fail to understand not because of its baffling mystery (Mark) but because this, the centre of the whole thing, is God's plan and not theirs. They will only wake up to it when it has been completed and done, and that point is not reached definitely until Pentecost in Acts, though the risen Christ of the last chapters of the gospel begins to open their eyes to it. Apart from that characteristically 'temporal' explanation, the verse is still a reminder of the not-knowing which discipleship entails because it is an allegiance to the mysteriously hidden will of God, to something not yet complete or obvious.

18.35–19.10

35 Then, as he was approaching Jericho, it happened that there was a blind man sitting by the roadside, begging.

36 He heard the crowd passing and enquired what it was all about.

37 And they told him, 'Jesus the man from Nazareth is going past you.'

38 So he shouted out,
   'Jesus, Son of David, have pity on me!'

39 Those who were in front tried to hush his cries. But that made him call out all the more,
   'Son of David, have pity on me!'

40 So Jesus stood quite still and ordered the man to be brought to him. And when he was quite close, he said to him,

41 'What do you want me to do for you?'
   'Lord, make me see again,' he cried.

42 'You can see again! Your faith has cured you,' returned Jesus.

43　　And his sight was restored at once, and he followed Jesus, praising God. All the people who saw it thanked God too.

1　　Then he went into Jericho and was making his way through it.

2　　And here we find a wealthy man called Zacchaeus, a chief collector of taxes,

3　　wanting to see what sort of person Jesus was. But the crowd prevented him from doing so, for he was very short.

4　　So he ran ahead and climbed up into a sycamore tree to get a view of Jesus as he was heading that way.

5　　When Jesus reached the spot, he looked up and said to him,
　　　'Zacchaeus, hurry up and come down. I must be your guest today.'

6　　So Zacchaeus hurriedly climbed down and gladly welcomed him.

7　　But the bystanders muttered their disapproval, saying,
　　　'Now he has gone to stay with a real sinner.'

8　　But Zacchaeus himself stopped and said to the Lord,
　　　'Look, sir, I will give half my property to the poor. And if I have swindled anybody out of anything I will pay him back four times as much.'

9　　Jesus said to him,
　　　'Salvation has come to this house today! Zacchaeus is a descendant of Abraham,

10　and it was the lost that the Son of Man came to seek – and to save.'

The first of these stories comes from Mark, the second is Luke's own. In order to accommodate the Zacchaeus incident inside Jericho the blind man is healed before Jesus enters the city and not as he comes out, as in Mark. Both

men undergo a change, a repentance: one from blindness to
sight, the other from swindling to honesty.

In Mark the restoration of the blind man (there called
Bartimaeus) is symbolic of the disciples' awakening to God
in Christ. In view of the last verse of the preceding section
and the subsequent story of Zacchaeus, this surely carries
over into Luke, though he makes some minor adjustments.
Instead of hearing that Jesus is about, the blind man hears
the sound of a crowd – an imaginative and realistic touch.
His reaction to being healed is to praise God as well as to
follow Jesus. The people (Luke's term for the Jewish nation)
praise God too. The main points are the portrayal of Jesus as
one who opens men's eyes and of praise and discipleship as
the right response to his work.

Zacchaeus is a thoroughly Lucan character, well-off, shady,
little, unrespectable – yet responsive to Jesus. He belongs
to that suspect fringe of Judaism which plays such a telling
part in the book. There, for Luke, are the people whom
Jesus not only likes but chooses to stay with and eat with
because they are not too encumbered with their piety and
virtue to heed the gospel. Unlike the ruler of 18.18f.,
Zacchaeus makes his act of renunciation without even being
asked to do so. Other Lucan trade-marks are *today* (cf. 2.11,
4.21, 5.26, 22.61), *salvation* (1.69, 77), *descendant of Abraham* (13.16).
Verse 10 is a definitive statement of one of the themes which
he explored thoroughly in chapter 15.

19.11–27

11   Then as the crowd still listened attentively, Jesus went
      on to give them this parable. For the fact that he was
      nearing Jerusalem made them imagine that the kingdom
      of God was on the point of appearing.

12   'Once upon a time a man of good family went abroad
      to accept a kingdom and then return.

13 He summoned ten of his servants and gave them a pound each, with the words, "Use this money to trade with until I come back."

14 But the citizens detested him and they sent a delegation after him, to say, "We will not have this man to be our king."

15 Then later, when he had received his kingdom, he returned and gave orders for the servants to whom he had given the money to be called to him, so that he could find out what profit they had made.

16 The first came into his presence, and said, "Sire, your pound has made ten pounds more."

17 "Splendid, my good fellow," he said, "since you have proved trustworthy over this small amount, I am going to put you in charge of ten towns."

18 The second came in and said, "Sire, your pound has made five pounds."

19 And he said to him, "Good, you're appointed governor of five towns."

20 When the last came, he said, "Sire, here is your pound, which I have been keeping wrapped up in a handkerchief.

21 I have been scared – I know you're a hard man, getting something for nothing and reaping where you never sowed."

22 To which he replied, "You scoundrel, your own words condemn you! You knew perfectly well, did you, that I am a hard man who gets something for nothing and reaps where he never sowed?

23 Then why didn't you put my money into the bank, and then when I returned I could have had it back with interest?"

24 Then he said to those who were standing by, "Take away his pound and give it to the fellow who has ten."

25 ' "But, sire, he has ten pounds already," they said to him.

26 "Yes," he replied, "and I tell you that the man who has something will get more given to him. But as for the man who has nothing, even his 'nothing' will be taken away.

27 And as for these enemies of mine who objected to my being their king, bring them here and execute them in my presence." '

The main part of the story comes from Matthew 25.14–30, but whereas Matthew gives no reason for the man's departure, Luke does. The addition of verse 14 is possibly a memory of Archelaus who went to Rome in 4 B.C. to receive the kingdom of Judaea, vacated on the death of his father, Herod. Although the Jews sent a delegation to protest, he got it. All this, together with the executions at the end, could be lifted from the parable without doing it much harm. It is certainly Luke's own contribution, and serves to concentrate the story on Christ as the one who is to be rejected by the Jews but will return to deal out justice.

The introductory verse 11 is Luke's. He is particularly concerned to show his (? bourgeois) readers that Jesus is not a political revolutionary, although his advance towards Jerusalem with his band of followers might look like a bid for power. *Because he was nearing Jerusalem* hints that the city's overthrow is coming to mind. Luke is also chary of enthusiastic expectation of the end (cf. 17.23).

The rest of the story explains itself. The sums put in trust are much more modest than in Matthew and the same for each servant, which makes the tale simpler. The rewards are the political jobs in the king's gift. The moral is the importance of exploiting, sensibly and adventurously, whatever one has been entrusted with. The trouble with the timid servant is not that his theology is wrong: it is perfectly right.

But with the timidity characteristic of the anxious orthodox he prefers conservative preservation to risky ventures. For Luke he probably represents orthodox Jewry, and verse 27 is no doubt a reference to the mass executions of A.D. 70.

19.28–44

28 After these words, Jesus walked on ahead of them on his way up to Jerusalem.

29 Then as he was approaching Bethphage and Bethany, near the hill called the Mount of Olives, he sent off two of his disciples,

30 telling them,

'Go into the village just ahead of you, and there you will find a colt tied, on which no one has ever yet ridden. Untie it and bring it here.

31 And if anybody asks you, "Why are you untying it?" just say, "The Lord needs it."'

32 So the messengers went off and found things just as he had told them.

33 In fact, as they were untying the colt, the owners did say, 'Why are you untying it?'

34 and they replied, 'The Lord needs it.'

35 So they brought it to Jesus and, throwing their cloaks upon the colt, mounted Jesus on its back.

36 Then as he rode along, people spread out their coats in the roadway.

37 And as he approached the city, where the road slopes down from the Mount of Olives, the whole crowd of his disciples joyfully shouted praises to God for all the marvellous things they had seen done.

38 'God bless the king who comes in the name of the Lord!' they cried. 'There is peace in Heaven and glory on high!'

39 There were some Pharisees in the crowd who said to Jesus,

'Master, restrain your disciples!'

40   To which he replied,

'I tell you that if they kept quiet, the very stones in the road would burst out cheering!'

41   And as he came still nearer to the city, he caught sight of it and wept over it,

42   saying,

'Ah, if you only knew, even at this eleventh hour, on what your peace depends – but you cannot see it.

43   The time is coming when your enemies will encircle you with ramparts, surrounding you and hemming you in on every side.

44   And they will hurl you and all your children to the ground – yes, they will not leave you one stone standing upon another – all because you did not recognize when God himself was visiting you!'

The story, rich in Old Testament references, is taken from Mark with some important adaptations: verse 28 links it firmly to the preceding prophetic parable as if that were an overture for this. The note of joy is characteristically increased by the addition of verse 37 in which *praises to God* are the reaction to Jesus' powerful deeds; in verse 38 the suspect word 'king' is inserted; *peace in Heaven and glory on high* is an echo of the angelic acclamation at Jesus' birth – 'peace on earth' would not be appropriate here. Verses 39–44 are entirely Lucan. They silence the familiar pharisaic protest against Christian joy and link the rejection of Jesus to the catastrophe of A.D. 70 which is described in some terrifying detail; God's visitation, his coming to take care and account of his people, is a Lucan motif (1.68, 78 and 7.16).

The effect of all this is first to make the happiness and the light more brilliant, second to match it against a deeper darkness. The dramatic tension is screwed up by this conjunction of black and white. God's will for peace, joy and reconciliation comes up against the gloom of men who reject the joy (the Pharisees) and the blindness of men who drift into disastrous war. No resolution of the cheering or the tears is offered at this point.

Jerusalem

45 Then he went into the Temple, and began to throw out the traders there.

46 'It is written,' he told them, ' "My house shall be a house of prayer", but you have turned it into a thieves' kitchen!'

47 Then day after day he was teaching inside the Temple. The chief priests, the scribes and the national leaders were all the time looking for an opportunity to destroy him,

48 but they could not find any way to do it since all the people hung upon his words.

1 Then one day as he was teaching the people in the Temple, and preaching the gospel to them, the chief priests, the scribes and elders confronted him in a body

2 and asked him this direct question,

'Tell us by whose authority you act as you do – who gave you such authority?'

3 'I have a question for you, too,' replied Jesus.

4 'John's baptism, now – tell me, did it come from Heaven or was it purely human?'

5 At this they began arguing with each other, saying,

'If we say, "from Heaven", he will say to us, "Then why didn't you believe in him?"

6 but if we say it was purely human, this mob will stone us to death, for they are convinced that John was a prophet.'

7 So they replied that they did not know where it came from.

8   'Then,' returned Jesus, 'neither will I tell you by what
     authority I do what I am doing.'

The long journey, which began as far back as 9.51, is over
at last and the destination is reached – Jerusalem, city of
God's peace and city of destruction. Jesus enters the Temple
again, where we last saw him as a boy at 2.46. It is a great
moment for Luke, so to emphasize it he trims away Mark's
notes about Jesus coming and going between Jerusalem and
Bethany (Mark 11.11, 19, 27): the city is entered once for all.
He also reduces the cleansing of the Temple to a bare mini-
mum since he has already referred to its final destruction in
unambiguous terms and will do so again at 21.5–6. Like
Matthew he leaves out Mark's 'house of prayer for all
nations', aware that its destruction will give a different
character to the Gentile mission. In any case it is Jesus, not
the Temple, who is the light for the nations (2.32). By leaving
out Mark's fig-tree (he has dealt with it already, 13.6–9) he
gets a continuous dialogue and debate from 19.47 onwards in
which, following the example of Mark and Matthew, the
issues at stake in this last act of the drama are brought into
the open. The Temple is the grand and evocative setting for
the arguments which go on until the end of chapter 21, but
it is now a more ambiguous place than it was when Jesus
was first brought there by his parents – and it is doomed.
His ministry has shown up the cracks in the fabric of Judaism
which indicate its impending catastrophe, and these debates
reveal them even more clearly.

As usual, the people are for Jesus, which embarrasses the
Jewish authorities. At 20.1 Luke has added *preaching the gospel*
to Mark's account, so making the whole Christian mission
and message the issue at stake, not just Jesus' recent actions.
The sharp argument which follows, lifted from Mark, shows
Jesus at his characteristic game of questioning his questioners
and bringing matters of theory down to earth. Instead of

debating the question of authority he confronts them with an authoritative figure, John, and their reactions to him. If they cannot get that straight they will certainly not get him straight. Caught between their fundamentally dishonest refusal to commit themselves and the prospect of being lynched, they opt for agnosticism.

20.9–18

9 Then he turned to the people and told them this parable:

'There was once a man who planted a vineyard, let it out to farm-workers, and went abroad for some time.

10 Then, when the season arrived, he sent a servant to the farm-workers so that they could give him his share of the crop. But the farm-workers beat him up and sent him back empty-handed.

11 So he sent another servant, and they beat him up as well, manhandling him disgracefully, and sent him back empty-handed.

12 Then he sent a third servant, but after wounding him severely they threw him out.

13 Then the owner of the vineyard said, "What shall I do now? I will send them my son who is so dear to me. Perhaps they will respect him."

14 But when the farm-workers saw him, they talked the matter over with each other and said, "This man is the heir – come on, let's kill him, and the property will be ours!"

15 And they threw him out of the vineyard and killed him. What then do you suppose the owner will do to them?

16 He will come and destroy the men who were working his property, and hand it over to others.'

When they heard this, they said,

'God forbid!'

17 But he looked them straight in the eyes and said,
  'Then what is the meaning of this scripture –
   The stone which the builders rejected,
   The same was made the head of the corner?
18 The man who falls on that stone will be broken, and
  the man on whom it falls will be crushed to powder.'

The motives of Jesus' opponents are dramatized and exposed in this allegory from Mark. It is an allegory in the sense that, once we have grasped that the farm-workers are the Jews, the owner is God, his servants the prophets, and his son Jesus, then everything falls into place. This suggests that the tale is the work of Mark or someone else in the early church rather than Jesus – a sort of Christian comic-strip condensation of religious history from creation to doomsday. It suits Luke's purpose well and he makes few alterations. By having the son first thrown out and then killed he brings the story into line with the succession of events in Christ's passion (so does Matthew). The theme is the incorrigible refusal of the Jewish nation to heed its Lord which leads to that final show-down and turning to the others which is to be Luke's last scene of all (Acts 28.23–29). To the horrified *God forbid!* Jesus replies with Psalm 118.22 which proclaims the revolutionary nature of God's actions. Luke, like Matthew, adds references to Isaiah 8.14 (the stone of stumbling) and Isaiah 28.16 (the precious cornerstone). At Romans 9.33 we find Paul fusing these two texts about the reversal of fortunes: God's people left behind and the Gentiles claimed by him. At an early stage these were favourite texts for the first Christians. They witness to a disturbing fact: the thing which men reject as scandalous nonsense is the thing which they really need.

19   The scribes and chief priests longed to get their hands
on him at that moment, but they were afraid of the
people. They knew well enough that his parable referred
to them.

20 They watched him, however, and sent some spies into
the crowd, pretending that they were honest men, to
fasten on something that he might say which could be
used to hand him over to the authority and power of
the governor.

21   These men asked him,
'Master, we know that what you say and teach is right,
and that you teach the way of God truly without fear or
favour.

22 Now, is it right for us to pay taxes to Caesar or not?'

23   But Jesus saw through their cunning and said to them,

24   'Show me one of the coins. Whose face is this, and
whose name is in the inscription?'
'Caesar's,' they said.

25   'Then give to Caesar,' he replied, 'what belongs to
Caesar, and to God what belongs to God.'

26   So his reply gave them no sort of handle that they
could use against him publicly. And in fact they were so
taken aback by his answer that they had nothing more
to say.

27   Then up came some of the Sadducees (who deny
that there is any resurrection)

28 and they asked him,
'Master, Moses told us in the scripture, "If a man's
brother should die leaving a wife but no children, he
should marry the widow and raise up a family for his
brother."

29 Now, there were once seven brothers. The first married
and died childless,

30 and the second

31 and the third married the woman, and in fact all the
seven married her and died without leaving any children.

32 Lastly, the woman herself died.

33 Now, in this "resurrection" whose wife is she of these
seven men, for she was wife to all of them?'

34 'People in this world,' Jesus replied, 'marry and are
given in marriage.

35 But those who are considered worthy of reaching that
world, which means rising from the dead, neither marry
nor are they given in marriage.

36 They cannot die any more but live like the angels; for
being children of the resurrection they are the sons of
God.

37 But that the dead are raised, even Moses showed to be
true in the story of the bush, when he calls the Lord the
God of Abraham, the God of Isaac and the God of
Jacob.

38 For God is not God of the dead, but of the living. For
all men are alive to him.'

39 To this some of the scribes replied,
'Master, that was a good answer.'

40 And indeed nobody had the courage to ask him any
more questions.

41 But Jesus went on to say,

42 'How can they say that Christ is David's *son*? For David
himself says in the book of Psalms –

The Lord said unto my *Lord*,
Sit thou on my right hand,

43 Till I make thine enemies the footstool of thy feet.

44 David is plainly calling him "Lord". How then can he
be his *son*?'

Jesus' enemies are testing him out with catch questions.
Of the two answers, first the is more radically common-

sensical, the second more radically theological than they expected. Jesus then sets them a riddle, the riddle of his own identity, which gets no answer. In the next section he closes the argument by satirizing and condemning their hypocrisy.

Verse 20 is an expansion of Mark's narrative, which Luke is still using, emphasizing the duplicity of the Jewish authorities and their malevolence. What better tool to trap the victim than a question which must evoke some kind of sell-out, compromising either his patriotism or his political innocence? The former would loosen his hold over the people; the latter would ensure his death as an insurrectionist. Jesus' deft reply is a guide to Christian political responsibility in normal times but cannot be said to solve the problem in its acuter or more confused forms: a rule of thumb rather than a law.

The Sadducees were conservative in their theology, refusing the doctrine of resurrection which the Pharisees had made popular. They come to Jesus with a ludicrous question such as only people who treat theology as a parlour-game could invent. Jesus cuts through it and shows that the question of resurrection is a question about God, not technicalities. Luke emphasizes this by the contrast of the two ages which he adds in verses 34 and 35. The basic error of the Sadducees is to confuse the conditions of earthly and heavenly existence. Luke has also expanded the end of verse 38 with *For all men are alive to him* (a quotation from the apocryphal 4 Maccabees 7.19, a pharisaical work of about the time of Christ). *A good answer* say the scribes, not because it answers the Sadducees' question on its own terms but because it recalls them to the real subject of theology: the living God.

Omitting the section in Mark about the great commandment because he has dealt with it already (10.25ff. – Good Samaritan), he moves on to the Son of David question. This is a riddle which Christians could put to Jews, arguing on the accepted ground of scripture. The answer to it has to be:

'David's son is David's Lord = Jesus Christ, the son of God descended from David.'

20.45–21.4

45   Then while everybody was listening, Jesus remarked to his disciples,

46   'Be on your guard against the scribes, who enjoy walking round in long robes and love having men bow to them in public, getting front seats in the synagogue, and the best places at dinner-parties –

47   while all the time they are battening on widows' property and covering it up with long prayers. These men are only heading for deeper damnation.'

1   Then he looked up and saw the rich people dropping their gifts into the treasury,

2   and he noticed a poor widow drop in two coppers,

3   and he commented,
    'I assure you that this poor widow has put in more than all of them,

4   for they have all put in what they can easily spare, but she in her poverty has given away her whole living.'

For this lampoon Luke follows Mark closely. He has already, in chapter 11, made use of Matthew's longer version. The rarity of the ability to write in the ancient world together with the prestigious connection of writing and religion in Judaism made the scribes into an important, not to say self-important, class. Jesus accuses them of using their honoured position as a screen for cruel dishonesty, the widow being the most vulnerable member of society.

Genuine piety is exemplified by a widow. The gifts of the rich cost them nothing and so mean little. The gift of this poor woman is *her whole living* and, costing so much, means much more. Though Luke does not say so directly here, we are dealing with a God who sees the inmost heart.

5 Then when some of them were talking about the Temple and pointing out the beauty of its lovely stone-work and the various ornaments that people had given, he said,

6 'Yes, you can gaze on all this today, but the time is coming when not a single stone will be left upon another without being thrown down.'

7 So they asked him,
'Master, when will this happen, and what sign will there be that these things are going to take place?'

8 'Be careful that you are not deceived,' he replied. 'There will be many coming in my name, saying "I am he" and "The time is very near now." Never follow men like that.

9 And when you hear about wars and disturbances, don't be alarmed. These things must indeed happen first, but the end will not come immediately.'

10 Then he continued,
'Nation will rise up against nation, and kingdom against kingdom;

11 there will be great earthquakes and famines and plagues in this place or that. There will be dreadful sights, and great signs from heaven.

12 But before all this happens, men will arrest you and persecute you, handing you over to synagogue or prison, or bringing you before kings and governors, for my name's sake.

13 This will be your chance to witness for me.

14 So make up your minds not to think out your defence beforehand.

15 I will give you such eloquence and wisdom that none of your opponents will be able to resist or contradict it.

16 But you will be betrayed, even by parents and brothers

and kinsfolk and friends, and there will be some of you
who will be killed

17 and you will be hated everywhere for my name's sake.

18 Yet, not a hair of your head will perish.

19 Hold on, and you will win your souls!

20 'But when you see Jerusalem surrounded by armed
forces, then you will know that the time of her devastation has arrived.

21 Then is the time for those who are in Judaea to fly to the
hills. And those who are in the city itself must get out of
it, and those who are already in the country must not
try to get into the city.

22 For these are the days of vengeance, when all that the
scriptures have said will come true.

23 Alas for those who are pregnant and those who have
babies at the breast in those days! For there will be bitter
misery in the land and great anger against this people.

24 They will die by the sword. They will be taken off as
prisoners into all nations. Jerusalem will be trampled
under foot by the heathen until the heathen's day is
over.

25 There will be signs in the sun and moon and stars, and
on the earth there will be dismay among the nations and
bewilderment at the roar of the surging sea.

26 Men's courage will fail completely as they realize what
is threatening the world, for the very powers of heaven
will be shaken.

27 Then men will see the Son of Man coming in a cloud
with great power and splendour!

28 But when these things begin to happen, stand up, hold
your heads high, for you will soon be free.'

29   Then he gave them a parable.

'Look at a fig-tree, or indeed any tree,

30 when it begins to burst its buds, and you realize without
anybody telling you that summer is nearly here.

31 So, when you see these things happening, you can be equally sure that the kingdom of God has nearly come.

32 Believe me, this generation will not disappear until all this has taken place.

33 Heaven and earth will pass away, but my words will never pass away.

34 'Be on your guard – see to it that your minds are never clouded by dissipation or drunkenness or the worries of this life, or else that day may catch you like the springing of a trap –

35 for it will come upon every inhabitant of the whole earth.

36 'You must be vigilant at all times, praying that you may be strong enough to come safely through all that is going to happen, and stand in the presence of the Son of Man.'

37 And every day he went on teaching in the Temple, and every evening he went off and spent the night on the hill

38 which is called the Mount of Olives. And all the people used to come early in the morning to listen to him in the Temple.

In Mark's gospel chapter 13 is the only place where Jesus has a long speech. It is characteristic of that troubled and troubling book that this should be about persecution and terror with the promise of final deliverance, the imminent sufferings of Jesus being linked to those of his followers. If Luke's gospel usually gives a more serene impression, it is not so in these present chapters. He can make good use of Mark's doom-laden discourse as the clouds gather and the quarrel between Jesus and his enemies sharpens towards violence. But Mark's version strikes him as being too wild. He makes alterations and additions which pin it down to history and emphasize the temporal sequence of the various horrors and then the final resolution, e.g. verse 6 *the time is coming*; the deceivers at verse 8 who say *The time is very near now*; *first* at verse 9; *But before all this happens* at verse 12; verses 20–24 which change Mark's vaguer calamity into a description of the Roman invasion and siege of A.D. 70. The insertion of *prisons* and *governors* at verse 12 is a glimpse of Acts, and possibly verses 25 and 26 look forward to Paul's alarming experiences at sea. Greater emphasis on God's controlling care is made by the addition of verses 15 (also referring to Acts), 18 and 28.

Mark's concluding trumpet-call 'watch!' is not clear or adequate for Luke. In verses 34–36 he adds sensible advice for his middle-class readership with its temptation to waste time on futile leisure or business worries. They will do better to pray so that they will not be weak and ashamed when the day comes and they confront their judge. This is more sober and economical than the string of parables which Matthew adds at this point. Verses 37–38 are also Luke's and bring us back to the Temple. By staying at night on the Mount of Olives, Jesus is in the suburbs of the city – in it but not of it, as it were.

There is a twofold structure: the time before the end which includes the doom of Jerusalem and the persecution and expansion of Christianity, and the time of the end. Luke is anxious that these should not be confused nor his readers unsettled by wild-eyed preachers proclaiming a premature end.

The reader should sit back and let the thing hit him with its full force, possibly reading chapters 13–23 of Josephus' *The Jewish War* (Penguin Classics) to get the aptness of it. This is not Old Moore's Almanack.

22. 1–22

1   Now as the feast of unleavened bread, called the Pass-over, was approaching,

2 fear of the people made the chief priests and scribes try desperately to find a way of getting rid of Jesus.

3 Then Satan entered into the mind of Judas Iscariot, who was one of the twelve.

4 He went and discussed with the chief priests and officers a method of getting Jesus into their hands.

5 They were delighted and arranged to pay him cash for it.

6 He agreed, and began to look for a suitable opportunity for betrayal when there was no crowd present.

7 Then the day of unleavened bread arrived, on which the Passover lamb had to be sacrificed,

8 and Jesus sent off Peter and John with the words, 'Go and make all the preparations for us to eat the Passover.'

9 'Where would you like us to do this?' they asked.

10 And he replied,
'Listen, just as you're going into the city a man carrying a jug of water will meet you. Follow him to the house he is making for.

11 Then say to the owner of the house, "The master has this message for you – which is the room where my disciples and I may eat the Passover?"

12 And he will take you upstairs and show you a large room furnished for our needs. Make all the preparations there.'

13 So they went off and found everything exactly as he had told them it would be, and they made the Passover preparations.

14 Then, when the time came, he took his seat at table with the apostles,

15 and spoke to them,
'With all my heart I have longed to eat this Passover with you before the time comes for me to suffer.

16 Believe me, I shall not eat the Passover again until all that it means is fulfilled in the kingdom of God.'

17   Then taking a cup from them, he thanked God and
      said,
          'Take this and share it amongst yourselves,
18   for I tell you that from this moment I shall drink no
      more wine until the kingdom of God comes.'
19   Then he took a loaf and after thanking God he broke
      it and gave it to them, with these words,
          'This is my body which is given for you: do this in
      remembrance of me.'
20   So too, he gave them a cup after supper with the words,
          'This cup is the new agreement made in my own
      blood which is shed for you.
21   Yet the hand of the man who is betraying me lies with
      mine on this table.
22   The Son of Man goes on his appointed way: yet alas for
      the man by whom he is betrayed!'

GENERAL NOTE

Way back at 9.31 we heard of the exodus Jesus had to fulfil
in Jerusalem. Now it is beginning in the setting of the feast
which commemorates the original Exodus – the days of unleavened bread and the Passover supper. Luke is still following
Mark and adapting him. His previous use of the anointing at
Bethany (7.36–50) leaves him with a cleaner narrative line.
He expands the story of the Passover supper by the addition
of teaching by Jesus, some gathered from Matthew and
Mark and some of his own. The table is, for him, more an
opportunity for talking than for eating. This has the effect of
making the episode a point of vantage and recollection in
which the church is consolidated for the future and the
perspective to the kingdom of God opened up in a traditional
Jewish setting. Using his favourite device of Jesus' table-talk,
he presents a quiet interior scene suffused by assurance and
hope before the bitter public drama of the trial and execution.

At 22.3 Satan reappears, taking up residence in Judas
Iscariot as a base of operations. He has been off-stage, apart
from the vision of his fall at 10.18, since 4.13 when he *withdrew
until his next opportunity* – and this, at last, is it. The end of verse 6
notes Jesus' popularity as the main difficulty for his enemies.
The motif is in Mark, but Luke underlines it as one would
expect in a popularizing book. He does little with the connecting incident of the preparation and finding of the room
beyond turning Mark's two disciples into Peter and John.
There is no sense in seeking a rational or plausible explanation of it. Here, as in Mark, it is a demonstration of Jesus'
divine knowledge.

The narrative of the supper begins with a solemn *when the
time came*, then goes straight into the meal and Jesus' words
about its significance. The prophecy of betrayal is put after
this – a reversal of Mark's order which makes for greater
clarity without slackening the drama. The words of Jesus in
verses 15–20 are certainly based on Mark, but thoroughly
altered. Verses 15–18 are Luke's own and set the meal as a
climax to what has gone before (*With all my heart I have longed . . .*)
and a gate into the future (*until all that it means . . .*): the time
theme again. The section from verse 19b (*which is given for
you . . .*) to the end of verse 20 may be a later addition to Luke's
work by a scribe who wanted to include the traditions of
1 Corinthians 11.24–25 and Mark 14.24 – perhaps because
these were used in his own church. Some old manuscripts
do not include these words, which are certainly at variance
with Luke's lack of salvation-theology about Christ's death.
We are back in undisputed Luke (freely adapting Mark) with
Yet the hand of the man . . . The shadow of betrayal falls suddenly
across the table – but Mark's terrible words 'It would have
been better for that man if he had not been born' are left out.

22.23–39

23   And at this they began to debate among themselves as to which of them would do this thing.

24   And then a dispute arose among them as to who should be considered the most important.

25   But Jesus said to them,

'Among the heathen it is their kings who lord it over them and their rulers are given the title of "benefactors".

26   But it must not be so with you! Your greatest man must become like a junior and your leader must be a servant.

27   Who is the greater, the man who sits down to dinner or the man who serves him? Obviously, the man who sits down to dinner – yet I am among you as your servant.

28   But you are the men who have stood by me in all that I have gone through,

29   and as surely as my Father has given me my kingdom,

30   so I give you the right to eat and drink at my table in that kingdom. Yes, you will sit on thrones and judge the twelve tribes of Israel!

31   'Oh, Simon, Simon, do you know that Satan has asked to have you all to sift like wheat? –

32   but I have prayed for you that you may not lose your faith. Yes, when you have turned back to me, you must strengthen these brothers of yours.'

33   Peter said to him,

'Lord, I am ready to go to prison, or even to die with you!'

34   'I tell you, Peter,' returned Jesus, 'before the cock crows today you will deny three times that you know me!'

35   Then he continued to them all,

'That time when I sent you out without any purse or wallet or shoes – did you find you needed anything?'

'No, not a thing,' they replied.

36   'But now,' Jesus continued, 'if you have a purse or
wallet, take it with you, and if you have no sword, sell
your coat and buy one!

37   For I tell you that this scripture must be fulfilled in me –
        And he was reckoned with transgressors.
So comes the end of what they wrote about me.'

38   Then the disciples said,
        'Lord, look here are two swords.'
        And Jesus returned,
        'That is enough.'

39   Then he went out of the city and up on to the Mount
of Olives, as he had often done before, with the disciples
following him.

The theme is the establishment of the Christian community. This was adumbrated back at 5.1–11 (the miraculous
catch of fish). Now the church is given its title deed and
charter. Its hierarchy and its constitution both reverse
worldly order. Luke draws on Mark 10.41–45, following its
sense rather than its exact wording and showing his knowledge of the secular world in the title of 'benefactors'. At verse 27
he takes his own line. Verse 28, also his own, gives a characteristic view of the community in terms of its past, present and
future – its continuity in history. At the same time verse 30
projects their present table-fellowship into the end of time,
making it an image of the great feast that God will then give
(Isaiah 25.6–8). The last half of verse 30 (you will sit on thrones) is
one of the few references to Matthew's gospel in these last
chapters (Matthew 19.28). Verses 31–33 are Luke's own. The
church, focused on Peter, is in for trouble at the hands of
Satan the accuser and disrupter. But Jesus has prayed for
him (cf. Hebrews 7.28). He will fail, but he will turn back to
his master and be the better able to strengthen his brothers.
Verse 33 with its references to prison and death gives a more

precise reference to Peter's future life than we get in the other gospels (cf. Mark 14.29). Verse 34 takes us back to Mark – and to the darkness of the more immediate future. Verses 35–38 are peculiar to Luke. They look back to 10.14. Life was easier then, but now the enemy has closed in for the kill. Jesus' reply in verse 38 is strange – surely ironical. Two swords are not going to help very much.

22.40–53
(omitting, with many ancient authorities, verses 43 and 44)

40   And when he reached his usual place, he said to them, 'Pray that you may not have to face temptation!'

41   Then he went off by himself, about a stone's throw away, and falling on his knees, prayed in these words –

42   'Father, if you are willing, take this cup away from me – but it is not my will, but yours, that must be done.'

45   Then he got to his feet from his prayer and walking back to the disciples, he found them sleeping through sheer grief.

46   'Why are you sleeping?' he said to them. 'You must get up and go on praying that you may not have to face temptation.'

47   While he was still speaking a crowd of people suddenly appeared, led by the man called Judas, one of the twelve. He stepped up to Jesus to kiss him.

48   'Judas, would you betray the Son of Man with a kiss?' said Jesus to him.

49   And the disciples, seeing what was going to happen, cried,
    'Lord, shall we use our swords?'

50   And one of them did slash at the High Priest's servant, cutting off his right ear.

51   But Jesus retorted,
    'That is enough.'
    And he touched his ear and healed him.

52 Then he spoke to the chief priests, Temple officers and elders who were there to arrest him,

'So you have come out with your swords and staves as if I were a bandit.

53 Day after day I was with you in the Temple and you never laid a finger on me – but this is your hour and the power of darkness is yours!'

Although Luke continues to use Mark he also continues to do so with sovereign freedom. The party moves to the Mount of Olives, not Gethsemane, the following of the disciples being emphasized. *Pray that you may not have to face temptation* is a reminiscence of 11.4 (Lord's prayer), put here (only by Luke) in order to bind together the trials of Jesus and his followers. To the same end he does not lay such heavy emphasis as Mark on the disciples' heedless sleeping and gives a sympathetic reason for it – emotional exhaustion. Verse 46 rounds off the incident and repeats its theme. Similar words occur here in Mark: Luke's contribution is to put them at the beginning too (verse 40) so that they frame the climax of Jesus' agony.

In his narration of Jesus' arrest Luke has again adapted Mark freely, omitting for clarity's sake his note about the arrangement Judas had made previously and the obscure incident of the young man running away naked (so does Matthew). His additions are: *Judas, would you betray the Son of Man with a kiss?* which adds pathos and dramatic intensity; the disciples' question at verse 49, another dramatic touch, and Jesus' words of restraint; the healing of the ear, which is a sign that throughout these terrible events Jesus will still be depicted as compassionate and reconciling; the introduction of the chief priests themselves at verse 52 so that Jesus can rebuke them directly; the strong last words of the passage which give a setting for all that follows. So Luke has humanized the story without weakening it. There is a certain lack of doctrinal punch since he sees the event of salvation in terms of the whole story, and particularly the resurrection and ascension, rather than in a stark focus on the passion alone (cf. 24.26). This will be his line throughout the passion narrative, particularly in his humane theme of Christ's tender mercy in the teeth of destruction.

22.54-71

54 Then they arrested him and marched him off to the High Priest's house. Peter followed at a distance,

55 and sat down among some people who had lighted a fire in the middle of the courtyard and were sitting round it.

56 A maid-servant saw him sitting there in the firelight, peered into his face and said,
  'This man was with him too.'

57 But he denied it and said,
  'I don't know him, girl!'

58 A few minutes later someone else noticed Peter, and said,
  'You're one of these men too.'
  But Peter said,
  'Man, I am not!'

59 Then about an hour later someone else insisted,
  'I am convinced this fellow was with him. Why, he is a Galilean!'

60 'Man,' returned Peter, 'I don't know what you're talking about.'
  And immediately, while he was still speaking, the cock crew.

61 The Lord turned his head and looked straight at Peter, and into his mind flashed the words that the Lord had said to him . . . 'You will disown me three times before the cock crows today.'

62 And he went outside and wept bitterly.

63   Then the men who held Jesus made a great game of
      knocking him about.
64   And they blindfolded him and asked him,
         'Now, prophet, guess who hit you that time.'
65   And that was only the beginning of the way they
      insulted him.
66   Then when daylight came, the assembly of the elders
      of the people, which included both chief priests and
      scribes, met and marched him off to their own council.
      There they asked him,
67   'If you really are Christ, tell us!'
         'If I tell you, you will never believe me,
68   and if I ask you a question, you will not answer me.
69   But from now on the Son of Man will take his seat at the
      right hand of almighty God.'
70   Then they all said,
         'So you are the Son of God then?'
         'You are right; I am,' Jesus told them.
71   Then they said,
         'Why do we need to call any more witnesses, for we
      ourselves have heard this thing from his own lips?'

  Mark's account, while remaining Luke's source, is given
another thorough overhaul. There is one meeting of the
Sanhedrin instead of two, and Peter's denial, instead of being
sandwiched between them, is put in front of the first and
more important one which remains. That meeting is itself
shorn of the black comedy of the false witnesses. Jesus is
not mocked in the council chamber by the dignitaries but,
more plausibly, by his guards in prison. We are thus given a
clearer and cleaner story: Jesus is taken off into custody at
night, Peter denies him, Jesus is interrogated in the morning.
Better informed than Mark about worldly matters, Luke
knows that the Jewish authorities were not allowed to exercise the death penalty. This, too, is a gain in clarity (Jesus is

condemned once instead of twice) though, as we shall see, it does not exculpate the Jewish leaders.

In verse 54 Jesus is led to the high priest's house rather than his prison, there he is put under guard and the reader's attention is free to focus on the scene with Peter. A loss in dramatic richness is the price Luke pays for easier reading, but he is left with drama enough and adds two telling touches of his own: *The Lord turned his head and looked straight at Peter* and the adverb *bitterly*. By being made three times, Peter's denial is thorough, complete and unqualified. It is also made from a position of comfort and relative security. But Peter's position is not easy. Satan, the accuser, is sifting him by means of these apparently innocent bystanders and no man is a match for such an adversary (verses 31–34 should be read again here, for they also show that Jesus' prayer and an overruling providence will not allow Peter's collapse to be final). Yet this does not detract from the bitterness of Peter's lie, nor from the fact that from now on Jesus faces alone the world's hatred (the Jews) and impotence to help (Pilate).

The cruelty of Jesus' guards is emphasized by the addition of verse 65. The trial, after some delay, begins with the crucial question for the Jewish authorities: is this the Christ, the fulfilment of their hopes, their ruler under God? But they do not really want to know: Luke makes that clear by his addition of *If I tell you, you will never believe me, and if I ask you a question, you will not answer me* to Jesus' reply. The situation with them is just as it was at 20.2–8 which is surely at the back of Luke's mind here. Luke has split the question in Mark 'Are you Christ, Son of the blessed one?' into two, one for each title. Jesus' reply to the first baffles them but also proclaims that the days of his *taking up into heaven* (9.51) are completed, for this is the day of his death, the day which ends an old era and begins a new one – hence *from now on*. The answer to the second question modifies Mark with *You are right* added to

I am, implying that the priests know the truth very well but cannot face it. Anyhow, Jesus' reply is enough and too much. He must go now.

THE CROSS

Luke's contribution is here more modest than Paul's, John's or Mark's. He wants to commend Christianity as the right religion for the world by means of a clear and attractive telling of its story. So he gives us an editing of Mark's dark and ambiguous narrative into something lighter and more intelligible: the good death of an innocent man. There are only hints of a theology of redemption. Instead such familiar themes as repentance, reconciliation, forgiveness and the fate of Jerusalem are dramatized. Jesus' innocence of the charges of sedition brought against him is underlined. The healing power still works in the teeth of destruction.

23. 1–25

1 Then they rose up in a body and took him off to Pilate,
2 and began their accusation in these words,
  'Here is this man whom we have found corrupting our people, and telling them that it is wrong to pay taxes to Caesar, claiming that he himself is Christ, a king.'
3 But Pilate addressed his question to Jesus,
  'Are you the king of the Jews?'
  'That is what you say,' he replied.
4 Then Pilate spoke to the chief priests and the crowd,
  'I find nothing criminal about this man.'
5 But they pressed their charge, saying,
  'He's a trouble-maker among the people. He teaches through the whole of Judaea, all the way from Galilee to this place.'
6 When Pilate heard this, he enquired whether the man were a Galilean,

7 and when he discovered that he came under Herod's jurisdiction, he passed him on to Herod who happened to be in Jerusalem at that time.

8 When Herod saw Jesus, he was delighted, for he had been wanting to see him for a long time. He had heard a lot about Jesus and was hoping to see him perform a miracle.

9 He questioned him thoroughly, but Jesus gave him absolutely no reply,

10 though the chief priests and scribes stood there making the most violent accusations.

11 So Herod joined his own soldiers in scoffing and jeering at Jesus. Finally, they dressed him up in a gorgeous cloak, and sent him back to Pilate.

12 On that day Herod and Pilate became firm friends, though previously they had been at daggers drawn.

13 Then Pilate summoned the chief priests, the officials and the people

14 and addressed them in these words,

'You have brought this man to me as a mischief-maker among the people, and I want you all to realize that, after examining him in your presence, I have found nothing criminal about him, in spite of all your accusations.

15 And neither has Herod, for he has sent him back to us. Obviously, then, he has done nothing to deserve the death penalty.

16 I propose, therefore, to teach him a sharp lesson and let him go.'

18 But they all yelled as one man,

'Take this man away! We want Barabbas set free!'

19 (Barabbas was a man who had been put in prison for causing a riot in the city and for murder.)

20 But Pilate wanted to set Jesus free and he called out to them again,

21 but they shouted back at him,

'Crucify, crucify him!'

22   Then he spoke to them, for the third time,
      'What is his crime, then? I have found nothing in him
      that deserves execution; I am going to teach him his
      lesson and let him go.'

23   But they shouted him down, yelling their demand
      that he should be crucified.
      Their shouting won the day,

24   and Pilate gave the decision that their request should be
      granted.

25   He released the man who had been imprisoned for riot-
      ing and murder, and surrendered Jesus to their demands.

   The trial before Herod, coming between the two interro-
gations by Pilate, gives variety and movement to the story.
The pattern of the passage is *a – b – a* with a mounting tension
going through it. Luke works freely from the outset. Only
verse 3 and bits of other verses are directly from Mark,
indicating that he is indebted to Mark for the general outline
of things but not their detail. This he provides himself. The
charge against Jesus is political ('Christ' is explained as meaning 'a king') and demonstrably false (see 20.20–26). Verse 2 is
marked by Luke's interest in Caesar (cf. 2.1) and verse 5 by
his sense of the progress and journey of Jesus' life. The scene
is a preview of the kind of misunderstanding that the apostles
will have to face in Acts (e.g. Acts 24.5) when vindictive
Jewish leaders bring them before neutral or friendly Gentile
magistrates. The shuffling from judge to judge is also like
Paul's experience.
   If the trial before Herod were historical it would surely
figure in the other gospels. It is unlikely that Pilate would
have played about like this: from other sources we know him
to have been a bold and bloody character. Other materials
than purely historical reminiscence lie behind it. These are:
1. Psalm 2, again quoted at Acts 4.26: 'The kings of the earth

set themselves, and the rulers take counsel together, against
the Lord and his anointed.'

2. Mark 15.16ff. where the Roman soldiers mock Jesus. Luke
exonerates them from this gratuitous cruelty and puts it on
to Herod's troops instead.

3. Ephesians 2.11–18 which describes the reconciliation of
Jewish man and Gentile man in the death of Christ. That
diagrammatic theology is here presented as a story with
verse 12 as its point.

The rest of the passage is concerned to clear the reputation
of Pilate (and thus the Roman Empire) as thoroughly as
possible. Pilate makes two extra declarations of Jesus' innocence, adding up to three in all. The possibility of the lesser
punishment of flogging at verses 16 and 22 also illustrates his
eagerness to let Jesus off somehow. The Barabbas business goes
to the wall as a result, being only patchily dealt with in verse
25. The last words of the passage almost suggest that it was
the Jews who crucified Jesus – a daring apologetic move, but
impossible history. Luke is not anti-semitic in our sense. He
is most likely a Jew himself, certainly a man soaked in the
Old Testament and appreciative of Jewish piety and customs.
But all along he has developed and intensified the theme of
how the Christ came to his own and they rejected him (cf.
John 1). The process by which the ancient people of God
disinherited themselves is a leading concern of both his books.
The adoption of Gentiles into the kingdom is its bright side.
Institutional religion with its age-old privileges and traditions
unconsciously cuts itself off from its own living source, and
the blessing passes to others, the poor of the nation first,
then the outsiders. The trial of Jesus is an irrevocable step in
this movement.

23.26–56

26   And as they were marching him away, they caught
      hold of Simon, a native of Cyrene in Africa, who was on

his way home from the fields, and put the cross on his back for him to carry behind Jesus.

27   A huge crowd of people followed him, including women who wrung their hands and wept for him.

28   But Jesus turned to them and said,

'Women of Jerusalem, do not shed your tears for me, but for yourselves and for your children!

29   For the days are coming when men will say, "Lucky are the women who are childless – the bodies which have never borne, and the breasts which have never given nourishment."

30   Then men will begin to say to the mountains, "Fall upon us!" and will say to the hills, "Cover us up!"

31   For if this is what men do when the wood is green, what will they do when it is seasoned?'

32   Two criminals were also led out with him for execu-
33   tion, and when they came to the place called The Skull, they crucified him with the criminals, one on either side of him.

34   But Jesus himself was saying,

'Father, forgive them; they do not know what they are doing.'

Then they shared out his clothes by casting lots.

35   The people stood and stared while their rulers continued to scoff, saying, 'He saved other people, let's see him save himself, if he is really God's Christ – his chosen!'

36   The soldiers also mocked him by coming up and presenting sour wine to him,

37   saying,

'If you are the king of the Jews, why not save yourself?'

38   For there was a placard over his head which read,

THIS IS THE KING OF THE JEWS.

39 One of the criminals hanging there covered him with abuse, and said,

'Aren't you Christ? Why don't you save yourself – and us?'

40 But the other one checked him with the words,

'Aren't you afraid of God even when you're getting the same punishment as he is?

41 And it's fair enough for us, for we've only got what we deserve, but this man never did anything wrong.'

42 Then he said,

'Jesus, remember me when you come into your kingdom.'

43 And Jesus answered,

'I tell you truly, this very day you will be with me in paradise.'

44 It was now about midday, but darkness came over the whole countryside until three in the afternoon,

45 for the sun's light was eclipsed. The veil in the Temple sanctuary was split in two.

46 Then Jesus gave a great cry and said,

'Father, I commend my spirit into your hands.'

And with these words, he expired.

47 When the centurion saw what had happened, he exclaimed reverently,

'That was indeed a good man!'

48 And the whole crowd who had collected for the spectacle, when they saw what had happened, went home in deep distress.

49 And all those who had known him, as well as the women who had followed him from Galilee, remained standing at a distance and saw these things happen.

50 Now there was a man called Joseph, a member of the Jewish council. He was a good and just man,

51 and had neither agreed with their plan nor voted for
   their decision. He came from the Jewish city of Arimathaea and was awaiting the kingdom of God.
52 He went to Pilate and asked for Jesus' body.
53 He took it down and wrapped it in linen and placed it
   in a rock-hewn tomb which had not been used before.
54   It was now the day of the preparation and the Sabbath
   was beginning to dawn,
55 so the women who had accompanied Jesus from Galilee
   followed Joseph, noted the tomb and the position of the
   body,
56 and then went home to prepare spices and perfumes.
   On the Sabbath they rested, in obedience to the commandment.

The 'they' of verse 26 appears to be the Jews – or, at least,
Luke leaves it open to the reader to take it that way. He adds
that Simon carried the cross *behind Jesus*, thus acting out the
discipleship of 9.23 and 14.27. These minor editorial touches
are followed by a larger Lucan insertion, the wailing women
of Jerusalem, which combines three of his interests: women,
the city, and the course of history. Once again the horrors of
A.D. 70 cast their shadow before them (cf. 14.41f.). Verse 30
quotes Hosea 10.8. The meaning of Jesus' words is plain: if an
atrocity like this can happen when things on the political
scene are going well, what will it be like when they go badly?
To the perceptive eye the catastrophe is not Jesus' but the
Jewish nation's, for Luke has tied the story of Jesus into the
run of international events.
   Similarly, Jesus' crucifixion is linked with the punishment
of two other unfortunates – Luke emphasizes this by altering
Mark to make the executions explicitly simultaneous.
Jesus' prayer for his tormentors is only in Luke and is very
like Stephen's words at Acts 7.60. It surely embraces the Jews
as well as the Roman soldiers since he has made them the

virtual executioners. There is a difference between the ordinary folk and the leaders: at verse 35 *the people* (for Luke = the Jewish people) *stood and stared* as if transfixed, while their rulers jeer – with greater insight than they know. Their words as they stand in Mark are emphasized and the soldiers repeat them at verse 37. The paradox of the helpless saviour (in John, the dying life-giver) goes deep into Christianity and life.

Verses 39–43 are very much Luke, the penitent criminal taking his place with other similar characters of this gospel such as the prodigal son, the unjust steward, the repenting publican, Zacchaeus and the prostitute. The reclaiming of the lost continues without interruption. The bitter words of his companion link this incident smoothly with the preceding mockeries. Paradise is the garden of the blessed dead – an image common to Jews and Christians at that time. This, much more than he asked for, is the criminal's reward.

Luke has thoroughly rewritten the death of Jesus, using Mark's work as little more than an outline. He omits the cry of desolation (Mark 15.34) and the passage about Elijah which follows it. The eclipse of the sun, actually impossible at Passover time, is a bold imaginative and symbolic stroke, which accounts for Mark's darkness. In Mark the rending of the veil is a climax coinciding with Jesus' death and representing the abolition of the barrier between the realm of God and this world. Here it takes a less striking position, the emphasis being transferred to the serene last words of Jesus in verse 46 which quote Psalm 31.5 with the addition of 'Father'. Only in Luke does the end come so gently: in Mark and Matthew it is despair, in John, triumph. Likewise the centurion's climactic and unexplained recognition 'Truly this man was the Son of God' becomes a lesser and more comprehensible assessment 'Certainly this man was innocent'. (Phillips' 'good' understood technically.)

From verse 48 the scene fades elegiacally. The penitent

breast-beating of the people is Luke's addition connecting with verses 27 and 35 before. Joseph of Arimathaea is a shadowy figure: like Gamaliel in Acts a sympathetic member of the Sanhedrin, like Anna (chapter 2) waiting for God's kingdom. Verse 54 provides a characteristic note of time. Verse 56 notes the proper ceremonies of burial and, in the customary Sabbath rest, probably echoes Genesis 2.2 with its sense of completion.

Luke's account of Jesus' death is quieter and less distressing than Mark's, without the theological depth of John's. But his main interests are woven into it: the compassion of Christ, the saving of the least and lost, the placing in the continuum of history. Because he is an historian in the sense of making worldly sense of things, his version has won the definitive place in most minds.

THE RESURRECTION

As with the cross, Luke's concern is to make attractive sense of something odd and fraught with dangerous possibilities. Here again Luke's gentler approach has its penalties as well as its charms. Does the matter-of-fact tone, the emphasis on the ordinariness and physical solidity of the risen Jesus, make the resurrection more, or less, credible? We must not make the naïve mistake of thinking that detail in a story means fact rather than fiction, nor forget that for Luke, like the rabbis and the Gentile moralists, doctrine can take the form of stories. Nor should we ignore the sovereign freedom with which he treats his source, Mark, which, if it were undiluted fact, or if he had our scientific reverence for hard fact, would be strange and even disgraceful. But we move in another world than the researcher's study: the world we enter as we go into the opera house, theatre or cinema, or open a novel – a place where physical and 'historical' facts are the scenery, the masks, by and through which something else expresses itself and touches us. These tales of a man returned from the grave, like the earlier tales of people and angels, are about the relations of our world with another. As the two touch, in the tale or in life, something happens which no words or colours can fix or fasten but only point to. Certainly, something 'actually happened' on Saturday night and Sunday morning, but just what is no longer accessible to us – if it ever was. Each gospel has a different version, even of the common material. To use Luke's lively and charming detail as scientific evidence is not the way to it. But listening to his stories, above all the walk to Emmaus, can still confront the reader with the power which then as now worked hiddenly but unmistakably.

24. I–II

1   But at the first signs of dawn on the first day of the week, they went to the tomb, taking with them the aromatic spices they had prepared.

2   They discovered that the stone had been rolled away from the tomb,

3   but on going inside, the body of the Lord Jesus was not to be found.

4   While they were still puzzling over this, two men suddenly stood at their elbow, dressed in dazzling light.

5   The women were terribly frightened, and turned their eyes away and looked at the ground. But the two men spoke to them,

'Why do you look for the living among the dead? He is not here: he has been raised!

6   Remember what he said to you, while he was still in Galilee –

7   that the Son of Man must be betrayed into the hands of sinful men, and must be crucified, and must rise again on the third day.'

8   Then they did remember what he had said,
9   and they turned their backs on the tomb and went and
     told all this to the eleven and the others who were with
     them.
10 It was Mary of Magdala, Joanna, Mary, the mother of
     James, and their companions who made this report to
     the apostles.
11 But it struck them as sheer imagination, and they did
     not believe the women.

Mark's work is being used here, but with such freedom that
it is little more than a point of departure for Luke's own
construction. It is some indication of what 'history' and 'fact'
were to a gospel-writer that at this point, where we would
hope for a scrupulous presentation of cool evidence, he
omits, adds, alters and generally pulls the thing about to
suit his purposes. The major difference is in the tone. In
Mark this section is explosively dramatic. The final picture
of people running, speechless with terror, from the scene of
God's action ends that disturbing book with an appropriate
bang. But Luke is not ending here, and he prefers orderly
exposition, step by step, to Mark's obscure thunder. So for
him this passage is an interim, in which the resurrection is
raised more as a question, in hints and guesses which will
be resolved by the appearance of Jesus later. At verse 3 they
enter and find no body before meeting the two men (one
only in Mark) – sensible order instead of sudden confrontation. In verses 5–8 the women begin to understand what
has happened as the two shining men explain it to them.
Mark's last verse is dropped. So is his prophecy by the young
man of the appearance of the risen Jesus in Galilee. All that
remains of it is the *while he was still in Galilee* of verse 6. For
Luke Galilee is far behind. Nothing more will happen there.
Jerusalem is the scene now and it is here, at the world's
centre, that the resurrection will move the story of Jesus into

the story of the church. But at the end of this passage it is still hanging in the air. (Verse 12 has been omitted because the author feels it is textually dubious.)

24.13-35

13 Then on the same day we find two of them going off to Emmaus, a village about seven miles from Jerusalem.

14 As they went they were deep in conversation about everything that had happened.

15 While they were absorbed in their serious talk and discussion, Jesus himself approached and walked along with them,

16 but something prevented them from recognizing him.

17 Then he spoke to them,

'What is all this discussion that you are having on your walk?'

They stopped, their faces drawn with misery,

18 and the one called Cleopas replied,

'You must be the only visitor to Jerusalem who hasn't heard all the things that have happened there recently!'

19 'What things?' asked Jesus.

'Oh, all about Jesus, from Nazareth. There was a man – a prophet strong in what he did and what he said, in God's eyes as well as the people's.

20 Haven't you heard how our chief priests and rulers handed him over for execution, and had him crucified?

21 But we were hoping he was the one who was to come and set Israel free. . . .

'Yes, and as if that were not enough, it's three days since all this happened;

22 and some of our womenfolk have disturbed us profoundly. For they went to the tomb at dawn,

23 and then when they couldn't find his body they said

that they had had a vision of angels who said that he was alive.

24 Some of our people went straight off to the tomb and found things just as the women had described them – but they didn't see *him*!'

25 Then he himself spoke to them,

'Oh, how foolish you are, how slow to believe in all that the prophets have said!

26 Was it not inevitable that Christ should suffer like that and so find his glory?'

27 Then, beginning with Moses and all the prophets, he explained to them everything in the scriptures that referred to himself.

28 They were by now approaching the village to which they were going. He gave the impression that he meant to go on farther,

29 but they stopped him with the words,

'Do stay with us. It is nearly evening and the day will soon be over.'

So he went indoors to stay with them. Then it happened!

30 While he was sitting at table with them he took the loaf, gave thanks, broke it and passed it to them.

31 Their eyes opened wide and they knew him! But he vanished from their sight.

32 Then they said to each other,

'Weren't our hearts glowing while he was with us on the road, when he made the scriptures plain to us?'

33 And they got to their feet without delay and turned back to Jerusalem. There they found the eleven and their friends all together,

34 full of the news –

'The Lord is really risen – he has appeared to Simon now!'

35   Then they told the story of their walk, and how they
     recognized him when he broke the loaf.

Here is one of Luke's best and most characteristic achieve-
ments, a short story whose spell-binding power comes about
by a controlled line, a sober realism and a muted sense of
wonder. It is his last great set piece, bringing together most
of the themes he has handled throughout the work, yet
with such skill that nothing strains or spoils the tale. Everything happens within it. That is typical of Luke, and so is the
conjunction of ordinariness and marvel at the climax of the
narrative, which so appealed to Rembrandt, the most Lucan
of painters. The only things like it in the New Testament are
the Prodigal Son, the Good Samaritan and the Christmas
stories – all Luke's.

A number of other features are trade-marks: the length,
the careful notes of time and of place in relation to Jerusalem
as centre, the emphasis on interior experience. The action
takes place on the road and at the supper-table – both Lucan
settings. Jesus is the fulfilment of old prophecy, himself a
powerful prophet, whose life is a progress through suffering
to glory – a very Lucan view. Because of all this, and the
dependence of verse 23 on Luke's edited version of his
Marcan source, it is likely that this tale is his own work,
influenced by Tobias' journey with the unrecognized angel
Raphael in Tobit. If he had any other source it has faded
under his colours and line, though the influence of the
earliest church services has left a mark on the wording of
verse 30.

A story is a story is a story. It cannot be boiled down to a
meaning. Here the power is in suggestion rather than outright doctrine: the risen Jesus unrecognized because of his
ordinariness, the moment of perception in the evening and
the habitual ceremonies of the table. 'He comes to us as one
unknown.' There is more here than a moral.

36   And while they were still talking about these things,
Jesus himself stood among them and said,
       'Peace be with you all!'

37   But they shrank back in terror for they thought they
were seeing a ghost.

38   'Why are you so worried?' said Jesus, 'and why do
doubts arise in your minds?

39   Look at my hands and my feet – it is really I myself! Feel
me and see; ghosts have no flesh or bones as you can see
that I have.'

41   But while they still could not believe it through sheer
joy and were quite bewildered, Jesus said to them,
       'Have you anything here to eat?'

42   They gave him a piece of broiled fish,

43   which he took and ate before their eyes.

44   Then he said,
       'Here and now are fulfilled the words that I told you
when I was with you: that everything written about me
in the Law of Moses and in the prophets and psalms
must come true.'

45   Then he opened their minds so that they could
understand the scriptures,

46   and added,
       'That is how it was written, and that is why it was
inevitable that Christ should suffer, and rise from the
dead on the third day.

47   So must the change of heart which leads to the forgiveness of sins be proclaimed in his name to all nations,
beginning at Jerusalem.

48   'You are eye-witnesses of these things.

49   Now I hand over to you the promise of my Father. Stay
in the City, then, until you are clothed with power
from on high.'

50 Then he led them outside as far as Bethany, where he blessed them with uplifted hands.

51 While he was in the act of blessing them he was parted from them and was carried up to Heaven. They worshipped him,

52 and turned back to Jerusalem with great joy,

53 and spent their days in the Temple, praising God.

The conclusion of the book is an anticlimax after the Emmaus story. It cannot be a resounding end because Acts is to follow: a future of which verses 47–49 are promises. Things are left open, hanging in the air and waiting.

The passage is in two halves. The first is a resurrection appearance story, nothing like as good as the preceding one, with a heavy emphasis on the flesh and blood of the risen Lord. The second begins at verse 44 and is a last testament or charge from Jesus to his church followed by some vague action. The whole has some relation to John 20.19–23, these two gospels both contradicting Mark and Matthew by their setting in and around Jerusalem rather than in Galilee.

The earliest account of resurrection appearances, 1 Corinthians 15.3–8, reads like a collection of sudden, even ecstatic, visions. Mark and Matthew do little to alter this, but John and Luke have physical detail about hands and feet, honey and fish, touching and eating, which balances the sense of the tremendous. Underneath lies Luke's conviction that the Christian mystery makes sense in terms of this world and his desire to put it across as *the* sound faith for the sensible man.

As the first half fixes the Lord and the faith into the ordinary things of physical existence, so the second, just as typically, stitches them to the course of time. Verse 44 testifies to the fulfilment of a long past which now, at last, makes sense (verse 45). Verse 46 tells of the recent past and present. Verses 47–49 open up an immediate but boundless future for which the first Christians are given their commission (*witnesses*) and their task (promotion of a *change of heart* leading to forgiveness). But that is still to come, together with the God-given power to do it. Meanwhile they must stay put and wait. A rather vague and unconvincing description of Jesus' departure (*up to Heaven* is not in all ancient manuscripts) follows. This is the price Luke has to pay for laying everything out in temporal sequence. He cannot fade out, either explosively like Mark or softly like John. There has to be an ascension scene, an actual exodus of Jesus, in the story, and this puts an excessive strain on imagery and credulity.

Two favourite themes merge at the end: the note of joy in response to the divine deed in Christ and the return to the Temple in Jerusalem where it all began and where, before long, it will all start again.

Also available in the Fontana Religious Series

What is Real in Christianity?
DAVID L. EDWARDS

The author strips away the legends from Jesus to show the man who is real, relevant and still fascinating. A clear, confident statement of Christian faith taking account of all criticisms.

Parents, Children and God
ANTHONY BULLEN

This book attempts to guide parents in their role as Christian educators. How they may answer their children's questions, how they may meet their children's needs from infancy to adolescence, how they may pray with their children, how they may talk to their children about sex: these and other topics are dealt with.

Ethics in a Permissive Society
WILLIAM BARCLAY

Professor Barclay approaches difficult and vexed questions with his usual humanity and clarity, asking what Christ himself would say or do in our world today.

Dialogue with Youth
AINSLIE MEARES

'This is a first-class general introduction to the world of young adults. . . . (It) is in general terms which convey a wealth of valuable insight . . . a quantity survey which helps to identify and map out a field of personal encounter in which few are competent, many are hesitant, all are involved.'

Church Times

Also available in the Fontana Religious Series

The Divine Pity
GERALD VANN

Undoubtedly Gerald Vann's masterpiece. Many people have insisted that this book should not merely be read, but re-read constantly, for it becomes more valuable the more it is pondered upon.

The Founder of Christianity
C. H. DODD

A portrait of Jesus by the front-ranking New Testament scholar. 'A first-rate and fascinating book . . . this book is a theological event.' *Times Literary Supplement*

Science and Christian Belief
C. A. COULSON

'Professor Coulson's book is one of the most profound studies of the relationship of science and religion that has yet been published.' *Times Literary Supplement*

Something Beautiful for God
MALCOLM MUGGERIDGE

'For me, Mother Teresa of Calcutta embodies Christian love in action. Her face shines with the love of Christ on which her whole life is centred. *Something Beautiful for God* is about her and the religious order she has instituted.' *Malcolm Muggeridge*

Jesus Rediscovered
MALCOLM MUGGERIDGE

'. . . one of the most beautifully written, perverse, infuriating, enjoyable and moving books of the year.' *David L. Edwards, Church Times*

Also available in the Fontana Religious Series

Something Beautiful for God
MALCOLM MUGGERIDGE

'For me, Mother Teresa of Calcutta embodies Christian love in action. Her face shines with the love of Christ on which her whole life is centred. *Something Beautiful for God* is about her and the religious order she has instituted.'

Malcolm Muggeridge

Instrument of Thy Peace
ALAN PATON

'Worthy of a permanent place on the short shelf of enduring classics of the life of the Spirit.'

Henry P. van Dusen, Union Theological Seminary

Sing A New Song
THE PSALMS IN TODAY'S ENGLISH VERSION

These religious poems are of many kinds: there are hymns of praise and worship of God; prayers for help, protection, and salvation; pleas for forgiveness; songs of thanksgiving for God's blessings; and petitions for the punishment of enemies. This translation of the *Psalms in Today's English Version* has the same freshness and clarity of language, the same accuracy of scholarship based on the very best originals available as *Good News for Modern Man* and *The New Testament in Today's English Version.*

The Gospel According to Peanuts
ROBERT L. SHORT

This book has made a lasting appeal to people of all denominations and none. It has been read and enjoyed by literally millions of people. A wonderfully imaginative experiment in Christian communication.